The Divorce Myth

The Divorce Myth

J. CARL LANEY

BETHANY HOUSE PUBLISHERS
Minneapolis, Minnesota 55438

Scripture quotations are taken from the New American Standard
Version of the Bible, © The Lockman Foundation, 1960, 1962,
1963, 1968, 1971, 1972, 1973, 1975, unless otherwise noted.

Published by Bethany House Publishers
A division of Bethany Fellowship, Inc.
6820 Auto Club Road, Minneapolis, Minnesota 55438

Printed in the United States of America

Library of Congress Cataloging in Publication Data

Laney, J. Carl, 1948—
  The divorce myth.

  Bibliography: p.
  Includes index.
  1. Divorce—Moral and religious aspects.
2. Marriage—Moral and religious aspects.
3. Remarriage—Moral and religious aspects.
4. Marriage counseling. 5. Divorce mediation.
I. Title.
HQ824.L36   306.8'9   81-7690
ISBN 0-87123-892-6   AACR2

Dedicated to Nancy,
my wife for life
(Proverbs 31:27-29)

About the Author

DR. J. CARL LANEY was educated at the University of Oregon (B.S. in Public Administration), Western Conservative Baptist Seminary (M.Div. in Biblical Literature, Th.M. in Biblical Literature), and Dallas Theological Seminary (Th.D. in Bible Exposition).

Presently the Associate Professor of Biblical Literature and the Chairman of the Department of Biblical Literature at Western Conservative Baptist Seminary, he is also a member of the Evangelical Theological Society.

Dr. Laney has served as pastor of three churches and has authored seven books and many articles. He is married and the father of three children, and the family makes their home in Portland, Oregon.

Foreword

It is a brave author that will tackle the subjects of divorce and remarriage! But these must be discussed in a day when divorce is so prevalent, even among evangelicals.

This book sets forth the biblical teachings in a clear and straightforward manner. Alternate interpretations of key passages are fully discussed on the basis of careful research, causing the reader to consider soberly the author's conclusions, even though he may not want to agree with them.

The author also gives guidelines for applying the biblical teaching to particular situations without compromise and in love.

Dr. Carl Laney is well qualified to undertake this work both academically and professionally (doctorate in theology from Dallas Theological Seminary and presently professor at Western Conservative Baptist Seminary). His arguments and conclusions (which I personally commend) will have to be reckoned with by all who study these subjects.

Charles C. Ryrie

Contents

Introduction

My boyhood friend Tom died with a bullet through his heart. He had driven his VW to the top of a hill west of town, pointed a .22 caliber pistol to his chest and pulled the trigger. Why? What brought him to such despair?

Tom was an only child and a rather quiet boy. We frequently played together and enjoyed fishing for perch at an old slough near town. He was secure and well adjusted to life. Then his mother was stricken with an incapacitating illness. She could no longer be an active mother—or wife. During the course of her illness, the flame of love that had drawn Tom's parents together began to dim. Through Tom's high school years his father began to spend less time at home and more time at the office. Before long, he was going out with other women.

Tom's parents kept their marriage together for his sake—to provide him with a home and a family. But when Tom went off to college, their motivation to continue the marriage declined. Between Tom's first and second year at college, his parents sent him to Europe for the summer, and while he was gone they secured a legal divorce. His father then married another woman.

Tom never recovered from the shock of learning that his mom and dad were divorced. He attempted to replace the family security which divorce had shattered. He became involved with a young woman but soon became depressed over doing what he knew to be wrong. Tom's interest in school and social activities resultantly declined. Then, in a state of depression and despair, he drove to a hill overlooking the town and took his own life. Ironically, Tom's death accomplished what his life could not do: it brought his parents back together—at least at the funeral.

There is probably no one reading this book who has not been touched by the tragedy of divorce and its repercussions. Statistics bear this out. The United States Census Bureau reports that in 1920 there was one divorce for every seven marriages, in 1940 one divorce for every six marriages, in 1960 one divorce for every four marriages, in 1972 one divorce for every three marriages, and in 1977 one divorce for every two marriages. There were 1,130,000 divorces in 1978, an increase of 39,000 over 1977; provisional figures for 1979 show a gain of another 40,000 divorces. The divorce rate in the United States has continued to climb and nearly doubled between 1967 and 1977. If the present rate continues, there will soon be one divorce for every marriage.

Perhaps there has been divorce among your own relatives, among your close friends, or in your own family. Few Americans have not shed tears over, or endured the scars of, the tragedy of marital failure. Unfortunately, this rampant rise in the divorce statistics is not limited to the families of unbelievers, but includes homes of evangelical Christians. Over the past several years I have witnessed marital break-ups in the homes of Christian workers, theology students, pastors, and a seminary colleague.

A contributing factor in the increased frequency of divorce in Christian homes is the lenient position many pastors, teachers, and Christian writers take in dealing with this subject. While undoubtedly sincere in what they teach, many are more influenced by their *experience* in dealing with divorce than by the Word of God. Frequently a young pastor will perform a wedding for a divorcée before he has thoroughly considered what the Bible says about the subject. Then some time later the young pastor sits down to examine the teaching of Jesus on the matter of divorce and remarriage. Typically, he will assume he is right until proven wrong, so he concludes that divorce and remarriage is permitted under certain circumstances. His only other alternative is to admit his error and recognize its consequences in the lives of those whose wedding he performed. Few have the courage, humility, or integrity to take this course of action.

I understand the Bible to teach that marriage was designed by God to be permanent until death. In this book I will present a basically "no divorce" position which shows that, according to the Scriptures, marriage is a lifelong relationship. Many books dealing with divorce suggest that it is allowable under certain circumstances. My book uniquely shows how the clear teaching of Jesus, "What therefore God has joined together, let no man separate," is not contradicted elsewhere in the Bible. I will also explain how the "exception clause" found in Matthew's Gospel would have been understood in the contemporary Jewish setting in which Jesus spoke.

Before you dismiss me as a narrow-minded "fighting fundy," let me assure you that I did not come to this position overnight, and I don't expect you to either. My views have developed over years of studying and teaching the Scriptures. I only ask that you give these views a fair consideration. Keep on reading and see if my view doesn't best reflect the clear and consistent teachings of the Scripture.

I also want it understood that I am not "down" on divorced people. I have a close friend whose wife was previously married and divorced. Although we do not see eye-to-eye on the matter of divorce, we have discussed the issue and have shared good fellowship together over the years. I have the utmost respect for him, his position, and his lovely Christian wife. In this book I hope to reflect God's attitude toward divorce and divorced people. God never compromises the issue of sin. Yet He is in the business of loving, forgiving, and restoring all those who fail to match up to His righteous standards—*and that includes us all.*

In this book I want to help you examine God's Word and thus establish a biblical approach to divorce and remarriage. I would like you to search the Scriptures with me for God's answers to such questions as:

1. Are there any legitimate, biblical grounds for divorce (adultery, desertion, or mental cruelty)?

2. If a person is divorced before becoming a Christian, is he or she entitled to another marriage as a believer?

3. Should a man or woman divorce a second spouse in order to return to the original spouse?

4. Is a person who has been divorced and remarried living in a state of continual adultery?

5. Does a person who has not been previously married commit adultery should he or she marry a divorcée?

I do not expect that all will agree with my conclusions, but I do hope that this study will challenge believers to rethink their views on this contemporary moral issue. Our discussion of divorce and remarriage must not center on "What saith Shammai?" or "What saith Hillel?" but on *"What saith the Lord?"*

1

The Divine Institution of Marriage

Next to the days of my physical and spiritual births, June 5, 1971, remains the most significant day of my life. On that day in the presence of my friends and relatives I repeated these words:

"I, Carl, take thee, Nancy, to be my wedded wife, to have and to hold from this day forward, for better for worse, for richer for poorer, in sickness and in health, to love and to hold dear, till death do us part, according to God's Holy Word; thereto I pledge thee my love."

Although I had studied the subject of marriage, read many books, and received much counsel concerning this important step in life, I knew very little about marriage and the commitment that is involved. Only during the last several years have I really begun to understand this unique institution of marriage which joins a man and woman as one flesh. I have pondered the answers to such questions as: "Why did God create Eve?" "Why did God institute marriage?" "What is marriage according to the Bible?" In this chapter we will investigate the Word of God in order to discover answers to these and other questions.

The Creation of Man (Gen. 1:26-28; 2:7)

Since no newspaper reporter was present to observe the creation of the universe, God alone can tell us how the world began. Genesis 1-2 gives us that record. While some people assert that Genesis contains two creation accounts (1:1-2:4 and 2:5-25), it is better to understand chapter one as emphasizing the creation of the physical universe, and chapter two as detailing the creation of man and woman.

Genesis 1:24-31 records for us God's work on the sixth day of creation. On the sixth day God created animals to inhabit the earth—larger domesticated animals ("cattle"), reptiles and insects ("creeping things"), and wild animals ("beasts of the earth"). Then God said, "Let Us make man in Our image, according to Our likeness; and let them rule over the fish of the sea and over the birds of the sky and over the cattle. . . " (1:26). And so God created man as the crown and culmination of His creative work. Verses 26 and 28 form the twin bases for the central thought in verse 27. Here the Bible reveals three things. *First,* man is the creation of God, not the result of evolution. *Second,* man is fashioned in the divine image. Charles Ryrie suggests that the image of God involves man's appointed dominion over the earth and his capacity for moral action.[1] *Third,* man is created a sexual being—male and female; the two terms literally mean "the piercer" and "the pierced."

Genesis 2:7 further reveals that God formed or fashioned man from the dust of the earth, and then breathed into him the "breath of life." The "dust" cannot symbolize animal life and imply evolution, for man's body returns to this material when he dies (Gen. 3:19). The "breath of life" seems to be God's own vital breath that bestows the life which He himself possesses. Lifeless clay became animate by the breath of the Almighty God!

The Provision of Woman (Gen. 2:18-22)

God repeatedly recognized that His creation was good (1:4, 10, 12, 18, 21, 25, 31), but He acknowledged that it was *not good* for Adam to be alone (2:18). Adam recognized his own incompleteness when he named all the creatures of the earth—an exercise of his dominion and authority—and "there was not found a helper suitable for him" (Gen. 2:20). While man and woman together are deemed "very good" (1:31), man by himself is incomplete or "not good."

In order to rectify the "not good" situation, God declared, "I will make him a helper suitable for him" (2:18). God designed woman to be man's suitable helper, or literally, "a helper agreeing to him." The Jewish Talmud says, "God did not create woman from man's head that he should command her, nor from her feet that she should be his slave, but rather from his side, that she should be near his heart." Woman was not to be man's slave but rather his helper. The word "helper" (*'ezer*) is used of God in Psalm 33:20 and 146:5, so woman is obviously not an inferior being! She is man's counterpart, agreeing with him mentally, physically, and spiritually. She is divinely designed to assist man in all the activities of life, which include exercising dominion over creation, raising children, and worshiping God!

While Eve is created to be Adam's equal, two things in Genesis 2 suggest the priority of the male over the female. One is the order of creation. The fact that Adam was created first suggests his priority and authority over Eve. Paul makes the same point in his discussion of the conduct of women in 1 Timothy 2:13. The other is the fact that Adam named Eve (Gen. 2:23). The naming of the woman was an exercise of authority and indicates the priority of the man over the woman. Let me clarify that *priority* and *equality* are not mutually exclusive concepts. The woman is to submit to her husband even though she is his equal and fellow-heir of the grace of life (Eph. 5:22; 1 Pet. 3:7). Why? Simply because that is the divine order God has established for the home and family. Interestingly, the same order exists in the Trinity, as God is the head of Christ, so man is the head of woman (1 Cor. 11:3). Submission and priority do not suggest inequality, for Christ was submissive yet equal with the Father.

The Institution of Marriage (Gen. 2:23-25)

Imagine Adam's excitement as he beheld with sleepy eyes the most beautiful creature of God's creation. In verse 23 Adam speaks his first recorded words. With ecstasy in his voice he declares literally:

> *"This one at last*
> *Bone—my bones!*
> *Flesh—my flesh!*
> *This one shall be called woman*
> *because from man this one was taken!"*

After Adam exercised his authority by naming the woman, God proceeded to establish the divine institution of marriage. The words of Genesis 2:24 are frequently construed as those of Adam. However, to attribute such foresight to Adam concerning marriage and family life seems hardly feasible. The New Testament helps us at this point. In Matthew 19:4-5 we read, "He who created them from the beginning made them male and female, and said, 'For this cause a man shall leave his father and mother, and shall cleave to his wife, and the two shall become one flesh.' " The words of Genesis 2:24 are quite clearly not those of Adam, but the words of the Creator himself.

Genesis 2:24 is the only statement about marriage which is repeated four times in the Bible. It appears first in the creation account of Genesis, then later in the context of Jesus' teaching on divorce (Matt. 19:5; Mark 10:7), and finally in Paul's illustration of the mystery of the church (Eph. 5:31). The verse has three parts and mentions three things which are essential to marriage: to leave, to cleave, and to become one flesh.*

Leaving. God's plan for marriage first involves "leaving." The phrase "for this cause" refers to verse 22. It could

---

* See Walter Trobisch, *I Married You* (New York: Harper & Row Publishers, 1971), pp. 12-20, for an insightful discussion of these matters.

be paraphrased, "that is why." Because God made woman, man is to leave his parents, with a view to establishing his own family. There can be no happy marriage without this first essential step.

When my little daughter, Elisabeth, was born, I was privileged to be in the delivery room and witness the amazing event. After the birth the attending physician took sharp scissors and cut the umbilical cord which bound Elisabeth to her mother. Was that a cruel, merciless act on the part of the doctor? No! We all knew it to be necessary for her growth and development. Just as a baby cannot grow up unless the umbilical cord is cut, so marriage cannot mature and develop unless the spouse separates from his or her parents in order to establish a new family.

Leaving is not always easy. It is often hard for children to leave their parents, and even harder for parents to let their children go. There are many marriages where the husband or wife is still "tied to mother's apron strings"—living under the authority of Mom and Dad. This allows marital interference by the in-laws and causes unnecessary tensions for the newly married couple. Someone has said that the two best legacies parents can give their children are roots and wings—the security of knowing that Mom and Dad are always there to help and encourage in time of special need, but also the freedom to live one's own life and develop one's own family.

The leaving does not, of course, suggest an abandonment of one's parents. The responsibility to "honor your father and mother" (Ex. 20:12) is applied by Jesus to adult Pharisees in Mark 7:6-13. In the context of caring for widows, Paul encourages believers to make some recompense or return to their aged parents—that is, provide for their needs (1 Tim. 5:3-4)! The Bible never suggests that the young couple avoid all contact with their parents, but that they "let go" of their former lives as a son and daughter in order to cement their partnership as husband and wife!

I remember the tears Nancy shed as we left her hometown shortly after our marriage to spend the summer in Santa Cruz, California, ministering to youth. There were days when Nancy was left by herself and felt quite lonely, but there was no way to return to the nest. Instead of turning to her parents and her former home, she had to turn to *me*. Together we began to develop a new life—a life that was neither hers nor mine, but *ours*!

Cleaving. The second essential ingredient for marriage is cleaving. "A man shall leave his father and his mother, and shall cleave to his wife." You cannot really cleave until you leave. There is a divine order in this process. They must leave for the purpose of cleaving and establishing a new home.

The Hebrew word for "cleave" suggests the idea of being glued together. It is used in Job 38:38 of dirt clods which stick together after the rain. It is used by Joshua of a military alliance (Josh. 23:12). The word is also used of the leprosy that would cling forever to dishonest and greedy Gehazi (2 Kings 5:27). In marriage, the husband and wife are "glued" together—bound inseparably into one solitary unit.

An interesting characteristic of glue is its permanence. Tape, on the other hand, is temporary. Only with great difficulty can two articles which are glued together be separated. If you try to separate two pieces of wood which have been glued together, you will discover that they usually don't separate at the joint. The glue holds the joint firm; the wood pulls away from its own grain and breaks! Items which are glued together cannot be separated without great damage. The same is true of persons "glued" together in marriage. It is a permanent relationship until death. There is no allowance made in Genesis 2:24 for divorce and remarriage.

You or I might have used the word "love" in place of "cleave," but God used a stronger word which would not be so affected by feelings and emotions. Cleaving *includes* love—*agape*—a sacrificial commitment patterned after Christ's own example of personal sacrifice (Eph. 5:2, 25).

Notice that the man is to cleave to "his wife." This indicates that God established marriage as a monogamous institution. But how can this be reconciled with the instances of polygamy recorded in the Bible? For example, Jacob had two wives (Gen. 29:15-30) and so did Elkanah, the husband of Hannah (1 Sam. 1:2). While at variance with God's ideal for marriage—one woman for one man—polygamy was allowed under Old Testament law in the case of a childless first marriage (cf. Deut. 21:15-17) and in the case of levirate marriage when a man married his brother's widow (Deut. 25:5-10). However, the practice never made for happy marriages, and on the contrary, brought great misery upon those involved (1 Sam. 1:6-7).

Cleaving to one's own wife would obviously exclude marital unfaithfulness. Being "glued" to one's wife and at the same time engaging in sexual intercourse with another woman are mutually exclusive concepts. Marital faithfulness is essential to the cleaving relationship.

Becoming one flesh. The third essential ingredient to marriage is, "they shall become one flesh." This phrase refers to the physical or sexual aspect of marriage. Becoming one flesh symbolizes the identification of two people with one community of interests and pursuits, a union consummated in the physical act of sexual intercourse. Although they remain two persons, the married couple becomes *one* in a mystical, spiritual unity.

Becoming one flesh does not in and of itself make a marriage. The leaving and cleaving must precede this. The leaving must be recognized by society for a marriage to exist. However, there is no sexual intercourse which does not result in two people becoming one flesh (1 Cor. 6:16)! A married man who has intercourse with a harlot has destroyed the uniqueness of the one-flesh relationship he enjoyed with his wife.

Notice that the verse says nothing about children. A

childless marriage is a marriage in every sense of the word. I believe that God sometimes withholds children in order to give them at a time that will glorify himself, or to enable a couple to have a ministry which would be impossible with the responsibilities of childrearing. However, while the couple may be one flesh without children, the procreation of and raising of children is an important aspect of marriage (Gen. 1:28). Yamauchi correctly observes, "This means, on the one hand, that sexual union in marriage is beautiful and honorable (Heb. 13:4), and on the other hand, that sexual gratification was not designed as an end in itself."[2]

The concept of "one flesh" is beautifully illustrated in the children God may give a married couple. In their offspring, husband and wife are indissolubly united into one person. My children, John and Elisabeth, possess my features and Nancy's; they are my flesh and my wife's. There is no way that I can retrieve my features from my daughter, nor could my wife retrieve hers. Something unique and permanent is formed when a child is born, and similarly when the one-flesh relationship is established in marriage.

Again, there is an order involved. Becoming one flesh—the physical union—follows the leaving and cleaving. In our modern promiscuous society the steps are often reversed. The Bible knows nothing of "trial marriages" where couples live together apart from wedlock. Premarital sexual intercourse is not only immoral, but it defrauds one's future spouse of the unique right of taking a virgin in marriage. Paul possibly speaks to the issue of premarital chastity in 1 Thessalonians 4:3-5 where he instructs the Thessalonians to abstain from sexual immorality and that each one should "possess his own vessel in sanctification and honor." There is some debate as to whether "vessel" refers to one's own *body* or one's own *wife*. The immediate context and 1 Peter 3:7 would argue for the latter view. The word rendered "possess" (*ktaomai*) means in Classical Greek "to acquire." Thus Paul could be referring to premarital chastity during courtship and the contracting of marriage! The male believer should court and take a wife in a pure and God-honoring way—not in the lustful passion and premarital sexual activity which frequently characterizes the relationships of unbelievers.

The Obligations of Marriage (Eph. 5:22-33)

Whenever I have performed a wedding, I have customarily instructed the bride and groom concerning their mutual obligations in the marriage relationship. This, I believe, is not only helpful for the bridal party, but also for the friends and family attending the wedding. I take my text from Ephesians 5:22-33. Here the Holy Spirit, through the Apostle Paul, gives some directives to husbands and wives, and reveals the symbolic purpose of marriage.

The wife: a submissive helper. The first command is for wives. Wives are commanded by Paul to submit to the leadership of their husbands as they submit to the Lord (Eph. 5:22). The words "be subject" simply mean "to place or rank under." The wife is to place herself under or in submission to her husband. When you want to hold up a vase of roses, you generally place a table under it. In the same way the wife is to "hold up" her husband in his work, ministry, and family responsibilities by placing herself under and being subject to him. This submission does not suggest inequality, for we remember that Christ was submissive to, but equal with, the Father (John 14:9; 17:4; Phil. 2:8). The submission of the wife to her husband is simply a part of God's overall plan for order in the family (Eph. 5:23-24).

The submission of the wife to her husband is not a matter of mere outward form, but of inner attitude. The wife can be a person of strong, even outspoken opinions, and still be submissive to her husband's authority if she respects him as the head of the home, and is prepared and content for him to make and carry out the final decision in all family matters. After the wife has made her thoughts fully known, she must be content to rest the matter with her husband and with God. It then becomes her responsibility to uphold her husband as he carries out the actions that must be taken.

Wives, don't chafe under your husband's authority. Rejoice in it. Be subject to your husband in all things. It is your special privilege to move under the protection of his authority! It is within this pattern of divine order that the Lord will bless you and make you a blessing to your husband, your children, your church, and your community!

The husband: a sacrificial lover. The second command is for husbands. Husbands are commanded by Paul to "love your wives, just as Christ also loved the church and gave Himself up for her" (Eph. 5:25). Ask the average husband, "Do you love your wife?" and he will reply, "Of course I do!" meaning what he feels toward her or perhaps what he does for her by way of care and consideration. The *agape* love that this passage of Scripture refers to, however, is not measured by what one feels or even by what one does. Rather, it is measured by the *sacrifice* of oneself as exemplified by Christ (Eph. 5:25-27). This is the love that is referred to in John 3:16: "For God so loved the world, that He gave His only begotten [i.e., unique or one of a kind] Son, that whoever believes in Him should not perish, but have eternal life." Because God loved the world, He gave His Son. Thus, when Paul writes, "Husbands, love your wives," he clearly means a love which is ready to sacrifice. The divine and spiritual authority of a husband over his wife must be rooted in the sacrifice of oneself.

Husbands, in loving your wife you must first care for her spiritual welfare. At home by prayer and word you must sustain her in spirit, strengthen her awareness of high and heavenly things, and advance her in Christian knowledge. Secondly, you must sacrifice for your wife and give yourself up for her. When a disagreement flares up in your marriage, it is your responsibility to humble yourself and ask forgiveness. This is death to the ego, for sometimes your wife's guilt may be as great or greater than your own. Yet you are called to love your wife as Christ loved the church, as He humbled himself under the guilt of sin "while we were yet sinners" (Rom. 5:8).

Finally, as a husband, you should exercise your authority over your wife with humility. The authority you have is not a right but a duty granted to you by God. This attitude of humility was demonstrated by Jesus Christ. The Apostle Paul writes, "Have this attitude in yourselves which was also in Christ Jesus, who, although He existed in the form of God, did not regard equality with God a thing to be grasped, but emptied Himself, taking the form of a bond-servant, and being made in the likeness of men. And being found in appearance as a man, He humbled Himself by becoming obedient to the point of death, even death on a cross" (Phil. 2:5-8). As a husband, *love* your wife! Follow the Lord Jesus in *sacrifice* and *humility*, and the transforming love of Christ will bless your home!

The symbolic purpose. As he concludes Ephesians chapter 5, Paul notes that there is a symbolic purpose of marriage. The marriage union is designed to reflect the relationship between Christ and His church (Eph. 5:32). Just as a union is formed in marriage when two people commit their lives to each other, so, too, a union is formed in salvation when a believer is joined to Christ. In marriage, then, it is not merely love which joins two people together in the sight of God and man, but the existence of a God-ordained union which is divinely designed to portray the intimate and inseparable relationship between Christ and His body—the church.

Summary and Conclusion

It is imperative that we understand marriage as God intended it to be. Only then will we have a straight edge by which to consider and evaluate divorce. On the basis of our study of God's Word, a number of observations may be made about the marriage institution.

1. *Marriage was instituted by God (Gen. 2:18, 24)*. He created a wife for Adam and ordained marriage because it was deemed "not good" for man to be alone. God created man a suitable helper to assist him in ruling the earth, raising a family, and worshiping God.

2. *Marriage is to be a monogamous relationship*. God gave Adam just one wife (Gen. 2:22). Polygamy was practiced during the Old Testament era, but this never made for happy homes and was not in keeping with God's original design.

3. *Marriage is to be a heterosexual relationship*. God created for Adam—a male, Eve—a female (Gen. 1:27, 2:22). There is nothing in Genesis about Adam and Bill! The command for procreation (1:28) points to the fact that God ordained the institution of marriage to be heterosexual.

4. *Marriage involves a formal and public leaving of one's own parents in order to establish a new family as a married couple (Gen. 2:24)*. The customs differ from culture to culture as to the ceremony or formalities involved. But there must be a public recognition of the couple's intent for a marriage to be recognized. This seems to be inherent in the concept of "leaving."

5. *Marriage is a relationship which binds a couple until death*. This is implicit in the concept of cleaving—being "glued together" or bound in one-flesh relationship. Jesus and Paul explicitly taught that the marriage relationship can be broken only by death (Mark 10:9; 1 Cor. 7:39; Rom. 7:2-3).

6. *Marriage involves the headship of the husband over the wife*. This is suggested by Adam's priority in the order of creation and in the naming of Eve. The headship of the husband is spelled out very clearly by the Apostle Paul in Ephesians 5:23 and 1 Corinthians 11:3.

7. *Marriage involves role relationships*. While the husband and wife are equal in spiritual privilege (Gal. 3:28; 1 Pet. 3:7), their divinely ordained roles in marriage differ. The wife is to function in the role of a submissive helper (Eph. 5:22-24), and the husband is to function in the role of a sacrificial lover (Eph. 5:25-28).

8. *Marriage is a divine vocation*. It is not a relationship to be entered into because of social pressure or parental compulsion. Paul recognized that both the calling to remain single and to be married were gifts from God (1 Cor. 7:7). Paul preferred the single life, for this freed him from family responsibilities which could distract his devotion to the Lord (1 Cor. 7:32-35).

Marriage is basically the legal union of a man and woman as husband and wife. Marriage is an honorable estate (Heb. 13:4) that God has ordained (Gen. 2:23-24) and Christ has blessed, as seen by His attendance at the wedding in Cana (John 2:1-11). Marriage can be a beautiful and happy experience for those who understand the institution as God ordained and designed it. However, God's plans for marriage as outlined in His Word are not always studied or followed. Unhappiness, discontentment, and marital disaster results. How do we speak to the issue of broken marriages? What happens when God's plan for marriage are not followed? What does the Bible say about divorce? The rest of this book will be devoted to these and related questions.

Study Questions

1. How would you explain the reason for the two different accounts of creation in Genesis 1-2?
2. What is the "image of God" in man (Gen. 1:27)? How has this image been effected by the Fall (Gen. 3; 1 Cor. 11:7; James 3:9)?
3. What circumstances preceded the creation of woman? Why did God make Adam a wife?

4. What indications are there in the creation of Adam and Eve that Adam was to be head over the woman?
5. Genesis 2:24 records God's words concerning the divine institution of marriage. What three major steps are involved in marriage? Explain them.
6. What significance do you see in the order of leaving, cleaving, and becoming one flesh?
7. What indications are there in Genesis 2:24 that God designed marriage to be a permanent and binding relationship.
8. What is meant by the phrase "become one flesh"? Is becoming "one flesh" the same as becoming married?
9. What roles has God given a husband and wife in marriage (Eph. 5:22-33)?
10. Explain the concept of submission in marriage. Does submission suggest inferiority? Why or why not?
11. How is a clear understanding of marriage, as God designed it, a deterrent to divorce?
12. How does God's plan for marriage compare with your own concept of marriage? If you are married, what truth from this chapter will you apply to make your own marriage stronger?

Notes

1. Charles C. Ryrie, *A Survey of Bible Doctrine* (Chicago: Moody Press, 1972), p. 105.
2. Edwin M. Yamauchi, "Cultural Aspects of Marriage in the Ancient World," *Bibliotheca Sacra* (July-September, 1978), p. 249.

2

The Teaching of Moses

Moses records in Genesis 2:23-24 that God's original design for marriage was one man with one wife for life (cf. Matt. 19:6). However, because of the Fall (Genesis 3), man has not always followed God's plan. In the pre-Mosaic period men were orally divorcing their wives as was the custom of heathen nations. Seeing something in his spouse that displeased him, a husband could simply say before witnesses, "I divorce my wife," or declare to his wife, "You are no longer my wife." The divorce would be final and the rejected wife would have no recourse but to leave her home. She was entitled to none of her husband's property. Only her apparel—the clothes on her back—could be taken with her. For this reason, coins on the headgear, rings, and jewelry became an important resource for the divorced woman.[1]

The problem facing Moses was that the absence of any divorce regulations actually encouraged rampant divorce. Men were divorcing their wives for a "weekend fling" and then taking them back again when the dirty laundry had piled up and the house needed cleaning! It was in light of this situation that Moses delivered God's legislation recorded in Deuteronomy 24:1-4.

It is crucial to understand that Deuteronomy 24 does not institute divorce! Divorce is "man made," not God ordained, and reflects man's sinful rejection of God's original plan for marriage. Deuteronomy 24 does not institute divorce, but treats it as a practice already known and existing.[2] This divine legislation given through Moses was designed to protect the rejected wife and to give her certain safeguards: (1) the possession of a divorce document; (2) the release from further domestic obligations; and (3) the freedom from interference by the former husband in the case of a subsequent marriage.

Grammatically, verses 1-3 specify the conditions that must apply for the execution of the specific directive of verse 4. *If* this is the situation (vv. 1-3), *then* this law must be followed (v. 4). This legislation really speaks to a particular case of remarriage after a second marriage, but the incidental information given about marriage and divorce in verses 1-3 is crucial to our understanding of what Moses required.

The Grounds for Divorce (24:1a)

When a man takes a wife and marries her, and it happens that she finds no favor in his eyes because he has found some indecency in her. . . .

When the wife of a married man loses his favor because of "some indecency in her," the husband is implicitly allowed to put his wife away. Notice that divorce is not demanded or even encouraged, but simply allowed. It is assumed that the husband would follow this course of action.

The precise meaning of the phrase "some indecency" (literally, "nakedness of a thing" or "a naked matter") is not clear and hence was the subject of rabbinic debates on divorce. Perhaps it refers to some physical deficiency—such as the inability to bear children. This may be suggested by a possible parallel between our text and an old Assyrian marriage contract.[3] More likely it refers to some shameful or repulsive act such as the indecency referred to in Deuteronomy 23:13 where the same expression is used as a euphemism for excrement.

There are several circumstances in the Old Testament

where divorce was not granted. Divorce was not granted in the case of adultery, for adultery was punished by death (Lev. 20:10; Deut. 22:22-24). Divorce was not allowed for a man who morally defiled his wife before marriage (Deut. 22:28-29), nor was it permitted in the case of a man who falsely accused his new wife of not being a virgin (Deut. 22:13-19). Apparently, however, according to Deuteronomy 24:1, divorce was allowed for some shameful act or indecency other than illicit sexual intercourse.

The Process of Divorce (24:1b)

. . . and he writes her a certificate of divorce and puts it in her hand and sends her out from his house. . . .

Moses required that if a man decided to divorce his wife, he was to write out a bill of divorcement and deliver it to her in person. The essential words of this document are, "Behold, you are free to marry any man."[4] A bill of divorcement which was in general usage among the Jews of the Diaspora suggests the sort of legal document that Moses required:

> On the _____ day of the week, the _____ day of the month _____, in the year _____ from the creation of the world, in the city of , _____ I, _____, the son of _____, do willingly consent, being under no restraint, to release, to set free, and to put aside thee, my wife, _____, daughter of _____, who has been my wife from before. Thus I do set free, release thee, and put thee aside, in order that thou may have permission and the authority over thyself and to go and marry any man thou may desire. No person may hinder thee from this day onward, and thou art permitted to every man. This shall be for thee from me a bill of dismissal, a letter of release, and a document of freedom, in accordance with the laws of Moses and Israel.
> _____ the son of _____, witness
> _____ the son of _____, witness[5]

The bill of divorcement was designed to protect the rights of the rejected wife, freeing her from any further responsibility to her husband. The divorce document also protected her from any interference by the former husband in the case of a subsequent marriage. This law undoubtedly checked the rampant divorce of Moses' day. The very process of having to write out a divorce document and then deliver it to the wife served to keep the husband from acting rashly or out of anger.

The process of divorce that Moses required discouraged divorce rather than encouraged it. Moses did not command divorce; he simply permitted it. He did require that a divorce document be written. Jesus explains in Matthew 19:8 and Mark 10:5 that the Mosaic concession with regard to divorce was due to the hardness of the Israelite hearts. Their hearts were hardened by their sinful rejection of God's original plan for marriage (Mark 10:9; Gen. 2:24).

The Prohibition Against Remarriage (24:2-4)

And she leaves his house and goes and becomes another man's wife, and if the latter husband turns against her and writes her a certificate of divorce and puts it in her hand and sends her out of his house, or if the latter husband dies who took her to be his wife, then her former husband who sent her away is not allowed to take her again to be his wife, since she has been defiled; for that is an abomination before the Lord, and you shall not bring sin on the land which the Lord your God gives you as an inheritance.

The main point of this legislation relates to a particular case of remarriage. Moses is saying that a man may not remarry his former wife if she has in the meantime married another man (v. 4). Even though her second husband should divorce her or die, she must not return to her first husband. To do so would be an abomination before the Lord and would bring the defilement of sin upon the land. This restriction seems to guard against divorce becoming a "legal" form of committing adultery.[6] The prohibition against remarrying the same woman undoubtedly acts as a moderating influence on divorce.

Conclusion

Moses, then, did not institute divorce, but acknowledged that it was taking place and sought to curb that which clearly contradicted God's original design for marriage. Granted, divorce did continue to take place, but it was never looked upon as a happy occasion. The lot of a divorcée was not pleasant (cf. Isa. 54:6). She was free to remarry, but not to a priest (Lev. 21:7), which indicates that a social or moral stigma was attached to her as a divorced woman. Generally a rejected wife returned to her home (Lev. 22:13). If she did remarry, she would never be permitted to return to her former husband.

Deuteronomy 24:1-4 indicates that when divorce did take place during the Old Testament period, a bill of divorcement was to be given to protect the rejected wife after marriage to another man. This does not alter God's original plan for marriage—one man with one wife for life (Gen. 2:24). It simply provides protection for the rejected wife when God's original plan for marriage is violated.

Study Questions

1. What was the situation facing Moses which led to the legislation of Deuteronomy 24:1-4?
2. Explain the grammatical structure of Deuteronomy 24:1-4. How does this help us to identify what is the essential message of the passage?
3. When was divorce permitted by Moses? Under what circumstances was divorce not permitted?
4. How would the requirement of writing a certificate of dismissal have discouraged divorce?
5. What would you identify as the main point of the legislation of Deuteronomy 24:1-4?
6. Why was remarriage to one's former husband after a second marriage forbidden?

7. What light does Matthew 19:8 and Mark 10:5 shed on
the Mosaic concession with regard to divorce?

Notes

1. Fred H. Wight, *Manners and Customs of the Bible Lands* (Chicago: Moody Press, 1953), p. 125.

2. Peter C. Craigie, *The Book of Deuteronomy*, The International Commentary on the Old Testament (Grand Rapids: Wm. B. Eerdmans Publishing Company, 1976), p. 305.

3. James B. Pritchard, ed., *Ancient Near Eastern Texts*, 3rd edition with supplement (Princeton University Press, 1969), p. 543.

4. *Gittin* 9:3.

5. *Encyclopedia Judaica*, 1971 ed., s.v. "Divorce."

6. Craigie, p. 305.

3

The Teaching of Ezra

How would you counsel a couple in the following hypothetical marital situation? Mike and Susan met in college and married while still unbelievers. Later Susan joined a neighborhood Bible study and eventually received Christ as Savior. As she began to grow in her new Christian faith, Susan became more and more repulsed by the conduct of her husband—drinking, smoking, and swearing. She valiantly attempted to lead Mike to Christ, but over a period of several years Mike became resentful of her "preaching at him" and refused to further discuss the matter of Christianity. Susan greatly desired to have a godly husband—one who would be the spiritual leader in the home. What should she do? She longed to have a husband who would pray with her, read the Bible with her, and take her to church. As she contemplated the options available to her, Susan considered divorce. A friend suggested that this might be God's will since Mike was an unbeliever, and God had told Israel to keep separate from the unbelieving Canaanites.

What would you say? Is there an Old Testament precedent for this course of action? Some people feel that Ezra 9-10 would suggest that divorce is a viable option for someone who is married to an unbeliever. A study of this text is in order.

The Historical Background of Ezra 9-10

It was under the decree of the Persian King Artaxerxes

(464-424 B.C.) that Ezra led a small group of Jewish exiles back to Jerusalem from Babylon in 458 B.C.[1] As has been prophesied by Jeremiah (25:11-12; 29:10), the Southern Kingdom of Judah had spent 70 years in Babylonian captivity because of the people's disobedience to the Mosaic Covenant (cf. Deut. 28:41, 63, 64; 2 Chron. 36:20-21). Now, under the edict of Cyrus (538-530 B.C.), the Restoration Period was in full swing (2 Chron. 36:22-23). In 537 B.C., 49,897 Jews returned to Jerusalem to rebuild the Temple (Ezra 2). While the Temple had been rebuilt, the matter of sacrificial worship was being neglected. The return under Ezra established worship in the Restoration Temple (Ezra 7:14-20).

Ezra, the scribe and leader of the second return, had been in Jerusalem about four and one-half months when the officials of the city brought to his attention a problem of major concern. Many of the Jews who had recently returned from Babylon had married the unbelieving Gentiles living in the land of Judah. Ezra was faced with the stark reality of mixed marriages between believing Jews and heathen Gentiles. What was he to do?

The Problem of the Mixed Marriages (Ezra 9)

> *The people of Israel and the priests and the Levites have not separated themselves from the peoples of the lands, according to their abominations, those of the Canaanites, the Hittites, the Perizzites, the Jebusites, the Ammonites, the Moabites, the Egyptians, and the Amorites. For they have taken some of their daughters as wives for themselves and for their sons, so that the holy race has intermingled with the peoples of the lands; indeed, the hands of the princes and the rulers have been foremost in this unfaithfulness. (Ezra 9:1-2)*

The civil authorities who informed Ezra of the failure of the Jews to keep separate from the heathen people made it plain that it was not merely a few ordinary citizens who were guilty, but rather the leaders of the people were the chief transgressors! Ezra knew that the intermarriage of

Jews with foreigners was strictly forbidden by the Mosaic Law because of the devastating consequences of such a practice. Marriage with an unbelieving heathen would almost inevitably result in worshiping heathen gods (Deut. 7:1-4; Mal. 2:11). This sin had plagued Israel during the period of the Judges (Judg. 3:5-6). Even Solomon with all his wisdom had succumbed to the temptation to marry foreign women, and as a result his wives turned his heart away to other gods (1 Kings 11:1-8).

Ezra understood fully that if the practice of intermarriage with foreigners continued, the Jews of the restoration community would soon lose their national identity and fall into idolatry (Ezra 9:2; Deut. 7:3-4). The people of Judah were on the verge of duplicating the very circumstances that led to the Babylonian Exile! Ezra responded quickly to this crisis. Out of intense concern for the situation, he inflicted himself in a manner customary of those in mourning (Ezra 9:3-4; cf. Lev. 10:6, Job 1:20, Ezek. 7:18).

At the time of the evening offering—between 2:30 and 3:30 p.m.[2]—Ezra arose from his humiliation to intercede for the people. He acknowledged his own shame (9:5-6) and Israel's great guilt (9:7-15). Ezra offered no excuses. He simply affirmed God's righteousness in contrast with Israel's guilt, and admitted that the nation was unworthy of anything except divine judgment (9:14-15).

The Abandonment of the Mixed Marriages (Ezra 10)

And Shecaniah the son of Jehiel, one of the sons of Elam, answered and said to Ezra, "We have been unfaithful to our God, and have married foreign women from the peoples of the land; yet now there is hope for Israel in spite of this. So now let us make a covenant with our God to put away all the wives and their children, according to the counsel of my lord and of those who tremble at the commandment of our God; and let it be done according to the law." (Ezra 10:2-3)

Ezra's prayer dramatically demonstrated his concern for the nation's sinful condition, and as a result the hearts of the people were changed. While Ezra was still praying in the Court of the Temple, a multitude of repentant people gathered to him (10:1). Although not among the offenders who had married foreign wives (cf. 10:18-44), Shecaniah represented the group. He confessed the nation's sin and proposed a solution to the problem (10:2-3). He recommended that the people covenant to put away their foreign wives. The term "put way" implies divorcement rather than legal separation, for the same word is used in Deuteronomy 24:2 where the context is clearly divorce. The divorces would be carried out "according to the law," a probable reference to the requirement of Deuteronomy 24:1-4 to provide the rejected wife with a certificate of divorce.

Acting on the suggestion, Ezra then issued a proclamation for the returned exiles to gather in Jerusalem; there he detailed their sin, commanded confession, and ordered the offenders to separate from their foreign wives (10:10-11). The people immediately affirmed their agreement with the proposal (10:12). Only four men opposed the plan as outlined in verses 12-14, but their opinion did not prevail (10:15). To facilitate Shecaniah's plan, judges were appointed to circulate through the nation and deal with the divorce proceedings individually (10:13-15). After a three-month investigation, seventeen priests, ten Levites, and eighty-six men of the congregation were found guilty. A total of 113 Jews were involved. While this figure is not as large as we might have expected, the situation was alarming because almost 25 percent of the offenders were religious leaders.[3] Each offender put away his foreign wife and offered a ram as a guilt offering according to the provision of Leviticus 6:4, 6 (cf. Ezra 10:19). God had used Ezra to preserve Israel's national identity and religious purity for at least one more generation.

The Reoccurrence of the Problem (Neh. 13)

In those days I also saw that the Jews had married women

> *from Ashdod, Ammon, and Moab. As for their children,*
> *half spoke in the language of Ashdod, and none of them*
> *was able to speak the language of Judah, but the language*
> *of his own people. (Neh. 13:23-24)*

Unfortunately, the temptation to intermarry continued to plague the restoration community. Later Nehemiah, who was appointed governor of Judah by Artaxerxes in 444 B.C. (Neh. 1-2), was forced to deal with the same problem. Although the people had pledged themselves not to give their daughters to the people of the land or take Gentile wives for their Jewish sons (Neh. 10:30), they again became unfaithful. It was probably during Nehemiah's absence between his first and second governorship (Neh. 13:6) that the people began to neglect the tithing and Sabbath laws (Neh. 13:4-22) and again became involved in mixed marriages with heathens (Neh. 13:23).

Following the example of the high priest's son who married the daughter of Sanballat the Horonite (Neh. 13:28), many Jews married Gentile women of the surrounding regions. This constituted a national crisis, for the children of these mixed languages had not learned the Hebrew language! Not only was the purity of the Jewish race again being threatened, but the Hebrew language was in danger of being forgotten.

Nehemiah took vigorous action against the offenders; he made them swear to abstain from intermarriage and, illustrating from the life of Solomon, warned them of the devastating consequences of such actions (Neh. 13:25-27). Nehemiah even chased off the son of Eliashib, the high priest. He was apparently expelled from the priesthood because the priestly line was not to be contaminated by intermarriage (cf. Lev. 21:6-8; 14-15). Nothing is explicitly stated in this passage about divorce, but it could be implied from Nehemiah's testimony, "Thus I purified them from everything foreign. . . " (Neh. 13:30). Perhaps this was accomplished by the process described in Ezra 10.

Conclusion and Application

Now, how does Ezra 9-10 relate to the issue of divorce and remarriage? This passage of Scripture records a unique situation in which divorce occurred and was in fact commanded when backslidden Jews married Gentile idolators. Such marriages violated the prohibition recorded in Deuteronomy 7:1-4, and the situation could be remedied only by separation. This was a unique attempt on the part of the leaders of the restoration community to keep the messianic line pure and the Hebrew faith uncontaminated as a result of mixed marriages with idolatrous heathen.

While such separation may seem harsh and undoubtedly caused unhappiness, especially for families with children (cf. Ezra 10:44), the continuation of the marriages would have undoubtedly resulted in idolatry. This would have resulted in the destruction of the recently restored nation (Deut. 7:3-4). In a sense, divorce was the only alternative. A. E. Cundall, Lecturer in Old Testament Studies at London Bible College, makes this helpful comment:

> The unhappiness caused by these broken homes must be set not only against the initial transgression involved in the contracting of the marriages, but also against the ultimate blessing to the whole world that could only come through a purified community.[4]

The action taken by Ezra and later by Nehemiah was necessary in the unique situation of the restoration community to preserve the nation.

How does this unique incident recorded in the Old Testament relate to the dilemma of Susan who is considering divorcing Mike, her non-Christian husband? Does the action taken by Ezra set a precedent for New Testament believers to follow? Three observations lead me to conclude that we should not attempt to apply this unique incident recorded in the Old Testament to modern marriages:

1. Ezra was concerned for the preservation of the Jewish

people as a separate and distinct nation, for it was from Israel that the Messiah would come (Gen. 49:10; Num. 24:17; Mic. 5:2), and through Israel that the Gentile nations would be blessed (Gen. 12:3). While God's concern during the Old Testament period was for the preservation of the people of Israel as a distinct nation, God does not seem to be similarly concerned to preserve the racial or ethnic purity of Gentile peoples during the age of grace (cf. Gal. 3:28). The facts which motivated divorce in Ezra 9-10 and possibly Nehemiah 13 would limit it to the unique conditions and settings of the Restoration Period.

2. In the Old Testament period we see that intermarriage would lead to idolatry (Deut. 7:3-4). Idolatry would result in judgment—possibly even exile from the land (Deut. 28:41, 63, 64). No such consequences are stated in the case of a mixed marriage between a Christian and a non-Christian. While Paul warns believers against making their closest associations with non-believers (2 Cor. 6:14-18), he points out that when such becomes the case in marriage, the unbelieving spouse is sanctified through the newly converted partner (1 Cor. 7:14). The presence of a believer in the home sets it apart and gives it a Christian influence it would not otherwise have!

3. Any tendency to make application of this unique incident in Ezra 9-10 to modern marriages, suggesting that a Christian should divorce an unbelieving spouse, would contradict the clear teaching of Paul in 1 Corinthians 7:12-13, "If any brother has a wife who is an unbeliever, and she consents to live with him, let him not send her away. And a woman who has an unbelieving husband, and he consents to live with her, let her not send her husband away." Paul plainly does not want believers to dissolve their marriages with unbelieving spouses!

It is interesting that nothing is said in Ezra 10 about remarriage for those who separated from their wives. One could assume that the Gentile wives remarried (cf. Deut.

24:1-4), and perhaps the Jewish men did as well. However, it would be unwise to draw any principle from this in light of the Scripture's silence on the subject. The divorce of the Gentile wives from their Jewish husbands is neither condoned nor condemned in this unique situation in the restoration community, but was apparently necessitated due to the devastating consequences of continuing the mixed marriages.

Study Questions

1. What sin had the Jews of the restoration community succumbed to in the time of Ezra (Ezra 9:1-2)?

2. What consequences of intermarriage with heathen were predicted by God in Deuteronomy 7:1-4? How were these fulfilled in Israel's experience (Judg. 3:5-6; 1 Kings 11:1-8)?

3. Outline Shecaniah's plan for dealing with the problem of the mixed marriages (Ezra 10:2-4). Was he suggesting divorce or separation?

4. Do you believe the Lord was using Shecaniah to lead Ezra to act on the matter of the mixed marriages? Why? Why not?

5. While the number of offenders was small, what points to the alarming nature of the situation Ezra faced?

6. The temptation toward intermarriage continued to plague the restoration community. What actions did Nehemiah take against the offenders (Neh. 13:25-28)?)

7. What motivated Ezra and Nehemiah to take such decisive action against intermarriage in the restoration community?

8. Why would it be wrong to make application of Ezra 9-10 to modern marriages, suggesting that a Christian should divorce an unbelieving spouse (1 Cor. 7:12-13)?

Notes

1. J. Staffold Wright, *The Date of Ezra's Coming to Jerusalem* (London: The Tyndale Press, 1948), pp. 23-28.

2. Alfred Edersheim, *The Temple: Its Ministry and Services* (Grand Rapids: Wm. B. Eerdmans Publishing Company, 1958), p. 144.

3. G. Coleman Luck, *Ezra and Nehemiah* (Chicago: Moody Press, 1961), pp. 72-73.

4. A. E. Cundall, "Ezra," in *The New Bible Commentary: Revised*, eds. D. Guthrie and J. A. Motyer (Grand Rapids: Wm. B. Eerdmans Publishing Company, 1970), p. 404.

4

The Teaching of Malachi

Kathy is a young mother—and a divorcée. She married as a non-Christian, but when her husband left her, she sought out help from the pastor of a local church. Through his counsel Kathy was led to trust Christ as Savior. She needs no one to tell her that divorce is wrong. She knows that divorce is a violation of God's plan for marriage. Her Catholic background and personal experience have only served to reinforce this view.

Kathy's major problem now is not so much accepting her divorce, but accepting herself. She once heard a radio preacher declare with zeal that according to the Bible, "God hates divorce." Kathy concluded from that sermon that God must then hate divorcées! Now Kathy is ill at ease among other believers who know of her divorce, especially among happily married Christian couples. She even has some difficulty praying to God!

How would you counsel Kathy? Does God really hate divorce? What is God's attitude toward divorcées? How should God's attitude toward divorced people be reflected in the lives of Christians? Malachi 2:10-16 speaks to these questions and related issues.

The Historical Background of Malachi

Between the first and second governorships of Nehemiah in Jerusalem, around 432-431 B.C., God raised up the prophet Malachi to protest the spiritual corruption into which the people had fallen. Malachi, whose name means "my messenger," exposed the causes of the spiritual declension and set forth the steps through which the Jewish community could be restored to fellowship with God. The prophet announced that "repentance is a prerequisite for blessing" (Mal. 3:7, 10-12). When Nehemiah returned from visiting the Persian King Artaxerxes (Neh. 13:6), he instituted reform and corrected the abuses Malachi had rebuked (Neh. 13:4-31).

In addition to their hypocrisy (Mal. 2:17) and neglect of tithes (Mal. 3:7-9), the people of Jerusalem had become involved in the scandal of mixed marriage and divorce (Mal. 2:10-16). This problem had been dealt with by Ezra (Ezra 10) and by Nehemiah during his first governorship (Neh. 10:30), but the ugly sin had appeared once again.

The Sin of Mixed Marriage (Mal. 2:10-12)

> *Do we not all have one father? Has not one God created us? Why do we deal treacherously each against his brother so as to profane the covenant of our fathers? Judah has dealt treacherously, and an abomination has been committed in Israel and in Jerusalem; for Judah has profaned the sanctuary of the Lord which He loves, and has married the daughter of a foreign god. As for the man who does this, may the Lord cut off from the tents of Jacob everyone who awakes and answers, or who presents an offering to the Lord of hosts.*

The Law of Moses specifically forbad all marriages with heathen as a safeguard against idolatry (Ex. 34:14-16; Deut. 7:1-4). Forgetting the severe consequences of such a practice, the Jews once again entangled themselves in mixed marriages.

Malachi begins in verse 10 by arguing that since God is Israel's Father and they are His children (Ex. 4:22), brotherly love should be shown one another and family loyalty upheld.[1] As it was, the Jews were dealing "treacherously" with one another by divorcing their Jewish wives in order to marry idolatrous heathen women (Mal. 2:11). The phrase "daughter of a foreign god" is packed with meaning, and refers to a woman of a foreign people who are dedicated to worshiping a heathen god. Such mixed marriages, says Malachi, profane God's covenant with the patriarchs, for they threaten Israel's distinctive faith and national existence. The sin also profaned the sanctuary (literally "the holiness") of the Lord (Mal. 2:11). What was profaned or made common was not the Lord himself, but those who were "holy" by virtue of their relationship with a holy God. The designation "holiness of the Lord" is a reference to God's chosen people (cf. Jer. 2:3; Ezra 9:2), not the Temple, as the NASB translation suggests.

In verse 12 Malachi calls upon the Lord for judgment upon all who profane the marriage relationship in this way. The phrase "cut off" means putting one to death (cf. Ex. 31:14). The universality of this divine retribution is evidenced by the expression, "everyone who awakes and answers." Not even the priests and Levites who officiate in Temple sacrifices and offerings are immune to the prophet's prayer for judgment!

The Sin of Divorce (Mal. 2:13-16)

And this is another thing to do: you cover the altar of the Lord with tears, with weeping and with groaning, because He no longer regards the offering or accepts it with favor from your hand. Yet you say, "For what reason?" Because the Lord has been a witness between you and the wife of your youth, against whom you have dealt treacherously, though she is your companion and your wife by covenant. But not one has done so who has a remnant of the Spirit. And what did that one do while he was seeking a godly offspring? Take heed then, to your spirit, and let no one deal treacherously against the wife of your youth. For I hate divorce, says the Lord, the God of Israel, and him who covers his garment with wrong, says the Lord of hosts. So take heed to your spirit, that you do not deal treacherously.

We discover in this section that the marriages of the men of Israel to the idolatrous women involved divorcing Jewish wives. Here God's messenger, Malachi, rebukes their sin. Nowhere else in the Bible is so much said concerning the evil of divorce!

The Israelites were distressed that God no longer accepted their offerings (Mal. 2:13). They actually expected a holy God to accept the worship of a sinful, unrepentant people! These Israelites failed to consider the sin which had incurred God's displeasure. The sin is specifically identified in verse 14—the violation of the marriage covenant with a wife taken in one's youth! Here we learn that God sees marriage as a covenant relationship (cf. Prov. 2:17)! Marriage is a partnership—a voluntary agreement which binds the two parties in a permanent relationship before God. The law of Hammurabi decreed that marriage was a legal contract to be drawn up with the appropriate documents, but for the Jews it was a *covenant* which the Lord witnessed (Gen. 31:50; Prov. 2:17) and for that reason was all the more binding.[2] God does not break covenants (cf. Lev. 26:40-45), and since divorce breaks the marriage covenant made before God, it does not meet with God's approval!

While verse 15 is a difficult verse to translate and interpret, it is clearly Malachi's intention to encourage husbands to remain true to their first wife. If one follows the translation of the New American Standard Bible, he interprets the verse to be setting forth a preventative against divorce. Interpreted accordingly, Malachi would be saying that none of the Jews having a remnant of the Spirit of God (or possibly "spirituality") had divorced their wives to marry foreign women.

However, if one follows the marginal reading of the NASB, he interprets the verse to refer to the original institution of marriage when God made two human beings one (Gen. 2:24)—with the specific purpose of giving them a godly offspring. In other words, while God had the creative power to make Adam any number of wives, He designed marriage to be one woman joined to one man, since polygamy and divorce are not conducive to raising a godly family. Not only, then, was the divine institution of marriage threatened by this epidemic divorce, but the future spirituality of the Jewish people was being endangered as well. When parents, on the other hand, remain faithful to their marriage vows, their children will enjoy the security and nurture which encourages godly living.

This second approach to the verse seems to better fit the concluding exhortation to remain true to one's wife, "Take heed then, to your spirit, and let no one deal treacherously against the wife of your youth," or don't deal treacherously by divorcing your wife. Rather, recognize the inviolable covenant relationship and remain faithful to the mutual pledges made before God!

Malachi concludes in verse 16 by expressing God's attitude toward divorce: " 'For I hate divorce,' says the Lord." Note carefully that God does not say, "I hate the *divorcée*!" Believers should not be hostile to those who have suffered a marital disaster, but should reflect Christ's attitude of loving concern. Recall our Lord's gracious dealings with the woman at the well who had been married five times (cf. John 4:6-26)! Divorce is likened by the Lord in verse 16 to covering one's garment with violence, a figurative expression for all kinds of gross injustice. This may refer to the custom of putting a garment over a woman to claim her as a wife (Ruth 3:9; Ezek. 16:8). Instead of spreading their garments as protection over their wives, those Jews had covered their garment with violence toward their wives.[3] In closing this section Malachi repeats his plea of verse 15, "So take heed to your spirit, that you do not deal treacherously." It is the fifth time in seven verses that Malachi has labeled the sin of divorce and mixed marriage as treachery!

Conclusion and Application

The prophet Malachi points out that it is in the best interest of both the family and community for marriage not to be broken by divorce. It is not only a violation of God's original plan for marriage, but divorce violates the marriage covenant to which the Lord is a witness! Divorce is treachery against life's most intimate companion and is a grievous sin which God hates!

So it's true! The Bible does teach that God hates divorce. But how is the verification of this truth going to help in counseling Kathy? She is already under a burden of guilt from her divorce. What shall we say to her? The key truth that Kathy needs to *know* and *experience* is that while God hates sin, He loves the sinner. This is clearly taught in John 3:16, "For God so loved the world. . . ." The "world" is the world of unbelievers—the billions of wicked people who are lost in their sins. God loved the world to the extent that He gave His unique Son, Jesus Christ, to die on the cross to redeem lost sinners.

The parables of the lost sheep, the lost coin, and the lost son in Luke 15 reveal God's attitude toward sinners. The Pharisees, to whom these parables were directed, thought that God hated sinners, but Jesus shows through His teaching that sinners are the special objects of God's affection. Kathy needs to know that God loves and accepts her just as she is—divorce and all! But that is not enough. Remember, I said that she needed to "experience" the truth that God hates sin but loves the sinner. Here is where you and I fit in. Believers, as ambassadors of Christ, are to reflect His attitude of loving concern and acceptance in dealing with people who have sinned against God. We need not (and must not!) compromise and call sin anything less than what it is. But we are to demonstrate Christ's compassion in dealing with those who have experienced marital failure. As Paul says, we are to "accept one another" (Rom. 15:7). This does not imply the approval of sin, but the acceptance of the sinner! Why? Because Christ accepted us—and died for us while we were yet sinners (Rom. 5:8).

Study Questions

1. What relationship do you see between the ministries of the governor Nehemiah and the prophet Malachi?
2. What two sins does the prophet Malachi rebuke in Malachi 2:10-16?
3. Explain the meaning of the phrase "daughter of a foreign god." How was mixed marriage with heathens a danger to the Hebrew faith (Ex. 34:14-16; Deut. 7:1-4)?
4. Malachi labels divorce as a violation of the marriage covenant with the wife taken in one's youth (2:14). What does the concept of a covenant relationship in marriage imply?
5. Explain the two possible approaches to Malachi 2:15. Which view is preferred and why?
6. What word is used repeatedly in Malachi 2:10-16 to refer to the sin of divorce and mixed marriage?
7. How would you describe God's attitude toward divorce as revealed in Malachi 2:10-16? What distinction should be made between God's attitude toward the sin and God's attitude toward the sinner?
8. How should God's attitude toward divorce and divorced people be reflected in the lives of Christians? Make some specific suggestions as to how believers might reflect God's attitude of love and compassion in dealing with divorcées.

Notes

1. Eli Cashdan, "Malachi" in *The Twelve Prophets*, The Soncino Books of the Bible, ed. A. Cohen (London: The Soncino Press, 1948), p. 345.

2. Joyce Baldwin, *Haggai, Zechariah, Malachi*, Tyndale Old Testament Commentaries (London: Inter-Varsity Press, 1972), p. 239.

3. Charles L. Feinberg, *The Minor Prophets* (Chicago: Moody Press, 1976), p. 258.

5

The Teaching of Jesus in Mark and Luke

The Dean of Faculty at the seminary where I teach recently convened a committee for preparing a statement on divorce and remarriage to which the faculty could agree. As the interaction on the subject began, it soon became apparent that there was a great diversity of views among the representative faculty members. As the discussion became more heated I declared, "I have it! There is one statement to which all the faculty can agree!" In anticipation my colleagues gave me their undivided attention. "The one statement to which all the faculty can agree," I said, "is that divorce and remarriage is a very tough subject!"

There was also a diversity of opinions on this subject in the time of Jesus, and while it remains a "very tough subject," it is not without biblical solutions. God did not give us His revelation to confuse us and lead us to many diverse conclusions in the practical areas of Christian life. Rather, His inspired Word is profitable for teaching doctrine, for reproving sin, for correcting wrong views, and for training in righteousness (2 Tim. 3:16). I believe in the doctrine of the perspicuity of Scripture—that the Bible is a clearly written book designed by God to be understood by men and applied to their lives. I would ask you now to put aside the diverse opinions of men and examine with me the teaching of Jesus on this all-important subject of divorce and remarriage.

The teaching of Jesus is really fundamental to any discussion of divorce and remarriage, for Jesus gives a divine perspective to the Old Testament concession (Deut. 24:1-4), and His teaching is the basis for the instructions of the Apostle Paul (1 Cor. 7:10, 12). The teaching of Jesus regarding divorce and remarriage is clearly presented in Mark 10:1-12 and Luke 16:18. What is not so clear is the meaning of the exception found in Matthew 5:32 and 19:9, which teaches that divorce and remarriage "except for *porneia*" is adultery. In this study we will allow that which is clear to illumine the passage which is more obscure. Accordingly, we will first examine the teaching of Jesus as recorded in Mark and Luke, and then in the next chapter consider the unique contributions of Matthew's Gospel.

It is important to establish at the outset that the two major passages containing the teaching of Jesus on divorce and remarriage (Matt. 19:1-12 and Mark 10:1-12) record the same incident. Both accounts have the same geographical setting (Matt. 19:1; Mark 10:1), the same audience (Matt. 19:3; Mark 10:2), the same question being asked (Matt. 19:3; Mark 10:2), the same Old Testament quotations (Matt. 19:4, 5, 7; Mark 10:4, 6-8), the same reply by the Pharisees (Matt. 19:7; Mark 10:4), the same rebuke by Jesus (Matt. 19:8; Mark 10:5), and the same subsequent incident (Matt. 19:13-15; Mark 10:13-16).[1] Because of these similarities it is doubtful that Matthew and Mark could be referring to two separate incidents. However, as we shall see, each gospel has unique contributions in its record of both the encounter with the Pharisees and the teaching of Jesus.

Since the more detailed teaching of Jesus is found in Mark, for the purposes of this discussion it will be most helpful to thoroughly examine Jesus' teaching in Mark 10:1-12 and then briefly consider the single statement in Luke 16:18.

The Question of the Pharisees (Mark 10:1-2)

And rising up, He went from there to the region of Judea, and beyond the Jordan; and crowds gathered around Him

again, and, according to His custom, He once more began
to teach them. And some Pharisees came up to Him, test-
ing Him, and began to question Him whether it was lawful
for a man to divorce a wife.

The geographical and historical background is crucial to
our understanding of this encounter between Christ and the
Pharisees. Jesus had concluded His Galilean ministry and
was now beginning His journey through Perea to Jerusalem
for the Passover and His own crucifixion. Traveling through
Perea in the spring of A.D. 33, Jesus was approached by
some Pharisees who sought to stump Him with a theological *test* question. Notice that the Pharisees were not asking
the question to learn but only to "test" Jesus. They actually wanted to get Him into trouble.

Only a year or two earlier John the Baptist, the forerun-
ner and introducer of the Messiah, had been imprisoned for
speaking out on the subject of divorce and remarriage
(Matt. 14:1-12). About A.D. 29 Herod Antipas, ruler of Gal-
ilee and Perea, visited his half-brother Herod Philip on his
way to Rome. As a result of this visit, Herod Antipas fell in
love with Philip's wife Herodias who was also Herod Antipas' niece! This sounds like a soap opera, but it is a true
story recorded for us by Josephus, the first-century Jewish
historian.[2] Herodias agreed to divorce her husband and
marry Herod Antipas under the stipulation that Antipas divorce his first wife. The two were then married in violation
of Mosaic Law (Lev. 18:16; 20:21).

John the Baptist wasn't afraid to rebuke sin—even in
high places. He declared to Herod Antipas, "It is not lawful
for you to have her" (Matt. 14:4)! Consequently, John the
Baptist was arrested and imprisoned in the east Jordan for-
tress of Machaerus.[3] Herodias was not content, however, to
leave John in prison, and when she had the opportunity she
arranged John's execution. At the request of her dancing
daughter, Salome, John's head was presented on a platter
at Herod Antipas' birthday party (Matt. 14:6-12).

Remember that the Pharisees had already determined

to destroy Jesus (Matt. 12:14; Mark 3:6). How to do it was the big question! Since Jesus was traveling through *Perea* on His way to Jerusalem, He was in the territory and under the jurisdiction of Herod Antipas. Undoubtedly the Pharisees were thinking, "If Herod Antipas arrested John the Baptist for speaking out against divorce and remarriage, perhaps he would do the same to Jesus!" They would use this "test" question on divorce to trick Jesus into making a statement against the marital affairs of Herod Antipas which would result in Jesus' arrest and possibly His execution.

The specific question addressed to Jesus centered on the meaning of the phrase "some indecency" in Deuteronomy 24:1. Divorce was accepted by virtually all Jews in Palestine during the time of Jesus on the basis of the regulation of Deuteronomy 24:1-4. There was a major controversy, however, over the legitimate *cause* for which one might divorce his wife.

The Jewish Mishnah, containing the oral traditions of Judaism, records the rabbinic debate for us:

> The school of Shammai said: A man may not divorce his wife unless he has discovered something unchaste about her, for it is written; Because he has found some unseemly thing in her (Deuteronomy 24:1). But the school of Hillel said: He may divorce her even if she spoiled a dish for him, for it is written, Because he has found some unseemly thing in her. Rabbi Akiba said: Even if he found another woman fairer than her, for it is written, And it shall be if she finds no favor in his eyes . . . . [4]

It is remarkable that although the same biblical text is cited—Deuteronomy 24:1—there is a radical difference in emphasis in the rabbinic views. The liberal school of Hillel said that divorce for any reason was legitimate, while the conservative school of Shammai allowed divorce only on the grounds of adultery. The question put to Jesus by the Pharisees was, "What side of the controversy are you on?"

The Concession of Moses (Mark 10:3-5)

And He answered and said to them, "What did Moses command you?" And they said, "Moses permitted a man to write a certificate of divorce and send her away." But Jesus said to them, "Because of your hardness of heart he wrote you this commandment."

Jesus knew the hearts of the Pharisees and responded with a counter-question that pointed them to the Mosaic Law which records God's original design for marriage. The Pharisees however, missed the point of the question, for they were more concerned with the *concession* of Deuteronomy 24:1-4 than the *command* recorded in Genesis 2:24! The Pharisees responded to Jesus' question concerning the command of Moses by citing Deuteronomy 24:1, "Moses permitted a man to write a certificate of divorce and send her away" (Mark 10:4).

Jesus then bluntly clarified the Mosaic concession before instructing the Pharisees concerning the original institution of marriage. Jesus explained that the Mosaic concession was due to the hardness of the hearts of the Israelites. To cope with their sinful and hard-hearted rejection of God's original design for marriage—one man with one wife for life—Moses required that a husband deliver to his rejected wife a divorce document. In no way did the legislation of Deuteronomy 24:1-4 institute divorce. The Mosaic Law was merely intended to regulate divorce and protect the rights of the rejected wife.

The Institution of Marriage (Mark 10:6-9)

But from the beginning of creation, God made them male and female. For this cause a man shall leave his father and mother, and the two shall become one flesh; consequently they are no longer two, but one flesh. What therefore God has joined together, let no man separate.

Jesus proceeded to instruct the Pharisees that divorce is actually alien to God's plan for marriage. In verses 6-9

Jesus draws from the Old Testament scripture four arguments against the principle of divorce.

1. *In the beginning God created one male for one female* (Mark 10:6; Gen. 1:27; 5:2). Had God wanted Adam to have a succession of wives, He would have created not only Eve, but Ellen, Sandra, and Joan!

2. Jesus appeals to Genesis 2:24 to point out that *marriage is the strongest of human bonds*—even stronger than filial relationships (Mark 10:7).

3. *In marriage two people actually become one flesh* (Mark 10:8; Gen. 2:24). The "one flesh" that the couple becomes in marriage is beautifully illustrated by the offspring that God is pleased to give them. A child partakes of the flesh of both the father and the mother, and the two are absolutely inseparable!

4. Jesus affirms that *God is the one who actually joins a couple in marriage, and what God has joined no man should separate* (Mark 10:9). The term for "joined together" means "yoked together," and the aorist tense points to the permanence of the bond. The phrase "let no man separate" is present imperative of prohibition and demands the cessation of something in progress (i.e., rampant divorce).[5] A good paraphrase of verse 9 would read, "Stop severing marriage unions which God has permanently bound together."

It is very significant that Jesus' conversation with the Pharisees ends with His affirmation of the permanence and inviolability of the God-ordained marriage union. He had fully answered the question of the Pharisees as to whether it was lawful for a man to divorce his wife. Jesus' answer to the Pharisees is quite clearly, "No!" Yet by making no application of His teaching to Herod Antipas, the ruler of the district through which He was traveling, Jesus avoided a confrontation which may have prematurely terminated His ministry.

The Clarification for the Disciples (Mark 10:10-12)

And in the house the disciples began questioning Him about this again. And He said to them, "Whoever divorces his wife and marries another woman commits adultery against her; and if she herself divorces her husband and marries another man, she is committing adultery."

Later that day when Jesus had found lodging for the evening ("in the house"), the disciples began to question Him again about the subject of divorce and remarriage (Mark 10:10). While Jesus had clearly stated that it was not lawful for a man to divorce his wife, Jesus' disciples were perhaps wondering as to the consequences of this sin.

Jesus declares to His disciples in no uncertain terms that divorce and remarriage by either the husband or the wife is *adultery* (Mark 10:11-12), a sin clearly condemned by God's moral law (Ex. 20:14; Deut. 5:18). Mere formal or legal divorce, according to Jesus, does not dissolve the actual marriage that was made permanent by God. Since God does not recognize divorce, the subsequent marriage of a divorced person would involve committing the sin of adultery against the rejected spouse.

Not only is divorce wrong because it separates what God has joined, but remarriage compounds the sin. A husband who divorces his wife and marries someone else is not only sinning against God, but also against his wife. He is involving himself in adultery "against her" (Mark 10:11). Mark records that the same rule applies to both the husband and the *wife*, a truth not revealed in Matthew's Gospel (cf. Matt. 19:9). Matthew was writing for Jews, among whom the divorce of a husband by a wife was so rare that the law made no provision for this possibility.[6] But what was exceptional among the Jews was very common among the Greeks and Romans. So, for the benefit of his Roman readers, Mark records the application of Christ's teaching to both the husband and the *wife*.

Thus, with a few simple words in Mark 10:1-12 Jesus refutes the view that divorce is a viable option for a married couple. He also refutes the rabbinical misinterpretations of the law and points the Pharisees back to God's original plan for marriage, upholding throughout the sacredness and inviolability of the marriage bond.

The Contribution of Luke 16:18

> *Every one who divorces his wife and marries another commits adultery; and he who marries one who is divorced from a husband commits adultery.*

At first glance, Jesus' teaching on divorce in Luke 16:18 seems unrelated to the immediate context. However, a closer examination reveals that verse 18 simply illustrates the point Jesus is teaching the Pharisees (Luke 16:14) in verses 16-17. Until the commencement of John the Baptist's ministry, the subject matter expounded by Jewish teachers and rabbis was the Law and the Prophets. But with John's preaching of the Gospel of the Kingdom (Matt. 3:2) and the announcement of the same message by Jesus (Matt. 4:17; Mark 1:15), some of the Pharisees mistakenly concluded that Jesus believed the Law and Prophets were over and done with. Jesus, however, emphasizes in Luke 16:17 that although He has announced the advent of a new order, this does not set aside God's law! The prophecies will be fulfilled down to the smallest detail, and the moral law of God remains absolutely authoritative.

Now, in verse 18 Jesus drives home His point with an illustration directed at the Pharisees who customarily sought to invalidate God's law by their own oral traditions (cf. Mark 7:13). The Pharisees were ignoring God's original design for marriage as revealed in Genesis 2:24 and allowing divorce on the most trivial grounds. Hillel thought that a burned supper was sufficient grounds for a divorce, and Rabbi Akiba went so far as to permit divorce if a man found someone prettier than his wife! Jesus says, "No! God's law outlasts heaven and earth!" Consequently, He affirms in verse 18 that everyone who divorces his wife and marries another commits adultery. In addition, Luke also records Jesus' teaching that anyone marrying a divorced person commits adultery.

Some have thought that in Luke 16:18 Jesus was publicly criticizing Herod Antipas who had divorced his wife to marry the divorcée Herodias. Thus he was guilty on both counts according to verse 18. However, while Jesus' words would certainly apply to Antipas, it is probable that they were aimed more at the Pharisees as the immediate context suggests (cf. Luke 16:14).[7]

Summary and Conclusion

While there may be a diversity of opinions among Christians on the subject of divorce and remarriage, there can be little debate over the clear teaching of Jesus as recorded in Mark and Luke. In Mark 10:1-12 Jesus refutes the views of the Pharisees and argues that marriage is indissoluble by divine institution (Mark 10:6), by the strength of the relationship (Mark 10:7), by the two becoming one flesh (Mark 10:8), by express command (Mark 10:9), and by the evil consequences resulting from divorce and remarriage (Mark 10:11-12). The teaching of Jesus in Mark 10:11-12 and Luke 16:18 is simply that divorce and remarriage by either the husband or the wife is adultery.

There are no exceptions recorded by Mark as he prepared his gospel for the Roman readers or by Luke as he wrote for the Greek Gentiles. It was a very strict view on divorce and remarriage that Jesus taught, for it contradicted the views held by both the liberal and conservative Jewish theologians of His day. Jesus held that since marriage is not a mere civil act, but a divinely ordained relationship, God alone has the right and power to appoint the beginning and end of marriage. Until a marriage is broken by the death of one of the partners, the couple should heed the words of Jesus, "What therefore God has joined together, let no man separate."

Study Questions

1. What evidence is there that Matthew and Mark record the same encounter between Jesus and the Pharisees on the subject of divorce?
2. How is the geographical and historical background of Mark 10:1-2 crucial for our understanding of Christ's encounter with the Pharisees?
3. Explain John the Baptist's position on divorce and remarriage. What resulted from his taking a stand on this issue?
4. What were the views of the rabbis in the time of Jesus on the subject of divorce and remarriage?
5. How does Jesus explain the Mosaic concession recorded in Deuteronomy 24:1-4 (Mark 10:4-5)?
6. What arguments are used by Jesus in Mark 10:6-9 to demonstrate that divorce is actually alien to God's plan for marriage?
7. Jesus declares that divorce and remarriage is adultery (Mark 10:11-12). Why does Matthew 19:9 apply this rule only to the husband while Mark applies it to both the husband and wife?
8. What unique contribution does Luke 16:18 make concerning Jesus' teaching on divorce and remarriage?
9. How did Jesus' teaching on divorce compare with that of the Jews of the first century? How does Jesus' teaching compare with that of twentieth-century teachers and preachers?

Notes

1. Robert H. Stein, "Is It Lawful for a Man to Divorce His Wife?" *Journal of the Evangelical Theological Society* 22 (June 1979), p. 116.

2. Josephus *Antiquities* XVIII 109-111.

3. Josephus *Antiquities* XVIII 116-119.

4. *Gittin* 9:10.

5. H. E. Dana and J. R. Mantey, *A Manual Grammar of the Greek New Testament* (Toronto: The Macmillan Company, 1927), pp. 301-02.

6. Josephus *Antiquities* XV 259.

7. Leon Morris, *The Gospel According to St. Luke*, Tyndale New Testament Commentaries (Grand Rapids: Wm. B. Eerdmans Publishing Company, 1974), pp. 251-52.

6

The Teaching of Jesus in Matthew

Two years ago a Christian friend (whom I will call Jim) was divorced by his wife. It was not really unexpected; their relationship had been deteriorating for several years. Jim was wholly devoted to his work, and his wife wanted a husband more devoted to developing a home and family life. Looking for companionship outside of her own marriage, Jim's wife began seeing another man and finally filed suit for divorce. This pattern is repeated all too frequently in Christian homes; so while I was saddened by this broken marriage, I was not terribly surprised. What interested me, however, was the change that took place in Jim's views on divorce and remarriage.

Prior to his unhappy personal experience, Jim held to a very strict view on marriage. He held that the relationship was "till death do us part." However, his personal experience began to affect his doctrine, and soon he began to modify his position and justify his divorce on biblical grounds. Since there was no confirmed evidence of adultery having taken place, he began to believe that Jesus permitted divorce for "emotional separation." He came to view his own divorce as having actually taken place when his wife stopped sleeping with him, six months before their separation, a full year before the divorce was legally finalized!

Generally speaking, Christians who divorce and remarry attempt to justify their right to do so by the Word of God.

Most frequently they appeal to the words of Matthew 5:32 and 19:9 to explain and justify their actions. "Divorce and remarriage is permitted in the case of adultery," they confidently affirm. Adultery is then defined as the physical act of sex outside marriage, the desire to have sexual relations outside of marriage (cf. Matt. 5:27-28), or even emotional unfaithfulness to one's spouse. While most of these Christians are honest and sincere in their convictions, sincerity is not really enough. I recall a "Peanuts" cartoon in which Charlie Brown was returning from a disastrous baseball game. The dejected Charlie Brown was muttering, "174 to nothing! How could we lose when we were so sincere?" Well, sincerity is not enough in either baseball or Bible doctrine. In spite of their sincerity, I believe that many well-meaning Christians are quite wrong in their understanding of what Matthew's Gospel teaches on divorce and remarriage. Therefore, a thorough investigation of the unique contributions of Matthew 5:31-32 and 19:1-12 are in order.

The Unique Contributions of Matthew

It is imperative to understand that Matthew's Gospel is uniquely and thoroughly Jewish in orientation. This is evidenced by the genealogy which traces Christ's lineage to David and Abraham (Matt. 1:1); by the emphasis on the fulfillment of Old Testament prophecy which the Jews would find meaningful (Matt. 1:22-23; 2:15, 17-18); and by the use of Jewish terminology such as "Son of David" (Matt. 1:1; 9:27; 21:9). Probably written around A.D. 50,* the Gospel of Matthew was designed to demonstrate and

---

*Clement of Alexandria (A.D. 144-220) mentions that the gospels with the genealogies (Matthew and Luke) were written first (Eusebius, *Historia Ecclesiastiça* 6.14), so the recent view of many modern scholars that Mark wrote first is probably in error. The "priority of Mark" is based on the questionable presupposition that Matthew had to borrow from Mark. Since the Jews would be the first who needed to know that the Messiah had come, Matthew wrote his gospel first, probably around A.D. 50.

convince Jews everywhere that Jesus of Nazareth is the promised Messiah of the Old Testament. Matthew repeatedly relates Old Testament messianic prophecies to the life and ministry of Christ, showing how they were fulfilled in the person of Christ.

Some have wondered why all the Lord's teaching on divorce is not recorded in Mark 10. Well, as Matthew wrote to Jewish readers, so Mark wrote for Roman readers.[1] Under the inspiration and guidance of the Holy Spirit, both selected from the teaching of Jesus that which would communicate and apply to their respective audiences. This is readily observed from the fact that Matthew makes frequent use of Old Testament quotations as compared to the relatively few Old Testament references in Mark's Gospel—the Romans had no appreciation for the sacred Scriptures. Mark explains certain Jewish traditions (cf. Mark 7:2, 11; 14:12) and translates Aramaic words (5:41; 7:34; 9:43; 14:36; 15:22, 34). To his Roman readers who were unacquainted with the Land of Israel, Mark explains the geographical relationship of the Mount of Olives and the Temple area (Mark 13:3).

An illustration of the differences between Matthew and Mark is found in the context of Jesus' teaching on divorce. Mark alone mentions the possibility of a woman divorcing her husband, "And if she herself divorces her husband and marries another man, she is committing adultery" (Mark 10:12). While Jesus clearly taught this truth, Matthew did not record it in his gospel to the Jews since Jewish law did not permit a woman to divorce her husband.[2] We see, then, that each gospel writer selectively recorded that teaching which would apply to his respective readers. It is in light of the needs of his Jewish readers, then, that Matthew makes several unique contributions to the teaching of Jesus on divorce and remarriage.

The first significant contribution of Matthew's Gospel regarding divorce and remarriage is found in the Sermon on the Mount (Matt. 5-7). In this sermon Jesus seeks to con-

vict the Jewish multitude of their need to find true righteousness in Him. Rejecting the Pharisaic standard of righteousness (Matt. 5:20), Jesus encourages inner conformity
to the spirit of the Law rather than mere outward conformity to the letter of the Law. In Matthew 5:31-32 we find
that while the Pharisees allowed divorce on the basis of the
Mosaic concession (Deut. 24:1-4), Jesus disallowed it but
for one exception! The clear contrast presented in Matthew
is between the Pharisaic interpretation of Deuteronomy
24:1 and Jesus' clarification concerning the permanence of
the marriage union.

Second, the response of the disciples to Jesus' teaching
reveals that they understood Christ's position to be quite
strict: "If the relationship of the man with his wife is like
this, it is better not to marry" (Matt. 19:10). Jesus went
beyond the "letterism" of the Pharisees to the spirit of the
Law. While divorce was *recognized* and regulated by Old
Testament Law, it was not *instituted* by Old Testament
Law. The disciples, who apparently had been following the
Pharisaic view of either Shammai or Hillel, recognized that
Jesus' teaching in essence allowed for no divorce! Their response was, "If you can't get out of marriage, it must be
best not to get married in the first place!" Jesus then declared that not all could accept this statement which affirmed a celibate life! He then instructed the disciples that
there were only a few who should not get married (Matt.
19:11-12). The point of His teaching was not to warn
against marriage, but to instruct concerning the permanence of the marriage relationship.

The third unique contribution of Matthew's Gospel is
the exception clause of 5:32 and 19:9 which teaches that divorce and remarriage "except for *porneia*" is adultery:

> But I say to you that every one who divorces his wife, ex-
> cept for the cause of unchastity [porneia], makes her com-
> mit adultery; and whoever marries a divorced woman
> commits adultery. (Matt. 5:32)

> And I say to you, whoever divorces his wife, except for im-

> *morality* [porneia], *and marries another commits adultery. (Matt. 19:9)*

While some would argue that these exceptive clauses are not part of the genuine teaching of Jesus but represent either an adaptation by Matthew or an interpolation by the early church,[3] there are no sound textual arguments against the genuineness of the clauses.* Therefore we will proceed under the premise that the exception clauses in Matthew 5:32 and 19:9 are authentic sayings of Jesus and part of the original text. The meaning of *porneia*, then, becomes the crucial question in discovering the teaching of Jesus on divorce and remarriage.

The Possible Meanings of Porneia

Unfortunately, many are so delighted to find one legitimate cause for divorce that this important Greek word—*porneia*—is given only superficial consideration. A study of the possible meanings of this crucial word has been long neglected.

Porneia is related to the noun *pornē* which is derived from the root "to sell." The original concept was to offer one's body for a price. The word *pornē* was especially used of slaves and meant "a harlot for hire."[4] From this comes the Greek word *porneia*, found in Matthew 5:32 and 19:9, which basically refers to unlawful sexual intercourse—"prostitution, unchastity," and "fornication."[5] It may also refer to sexual aberrations, for it is used in the contexts of homosexuality (cf. Rom. 1:29) and incest (cf. 1 Cor. 5:1). What, then, is the precise meaning of the phrase "except for *porneia*," recorded by Matthew in the context of Jesus' teaching on divorce and remarriage? Four possible views on

---

*See Bruce M. Metzger, *A Textual Commentary on the Greek New Testament* (London: United Bible Societies, 1971), pp. 13-14, 47-48.

the meaning of this phrase are deserving of our investigation.*

1. *Adultery or unlawful sexual intercourse*. The traditional and most popular interpretation of the exception clause is that Jesus is making an allowance for divorce in the case of a marriage where adultery has been committed. Some advocates of this position take the term as referring not only to adultery, but to *any* illicit or deviate sexual behavior. It is argued that the exception clause would allow for both divorce and remarriage since divorce implies the complete dissolution of the relationship and marriage bond. Jesus, then, would be siding with the conservative school of Shammai which allowed divorce only in the case of adultery. John Murray and Lorraine Boettner are advocates of this interpretation of the exception clause.[6]

While this interpretation has been accepted by many Christians, it is not without several serious difficulties. The first major problem is that this view contradicts the teaching of Jesus found in Mark 10:1-12 and Luke 16:18. The Roman readers of Mark's Gospel and the Greek-Gentile readers of Luke would not have known of this exception recorded only in Matthew's Gospel for Jewish readers. While twentieth-century Christians can read all three Synoptic Gospels and harmonize the passages, the early church—without the benefit of Matthew's Gospel—would understand Jesus to be teaching that divorce and remarriage results in adultery—without exception.

A second objection to this position is that it contradicts the teaching of Jesus in Matthew 19:6 where He makes the clear and solemn prohibition, "What therefore God has joined together, let no man separate." The present impera-

---

*For a very thorough survey see H. G. Coiner, "Those 'Divorce and Remarriage' Passages (Matt. 5:32, 19:9, 1 Cor. 7:10-16)," *Concordia Theological Monthly* 39 (June 1968), pp. 373-77.

tive of prohibition demands the cessation of something then in progress—the severing of marriage unions. We must interpret the more obscure phrase, "except for *porneia*," in light of the clear statement in verse 6. Whatever the exception in verse 9 refers to, Jesus must be found consistent with himself. He will not contradict His clear command of Matthew 19:6 to stop severing marriage unions which God has permanently bound together.

The third problem is that according to this interpretation, Jesus' teaching did not rise above that of Shammai and the Pharisees, contrary to His usual pattern (cf. Matt. 5:21-48). Christ customarily rebuked the superficiality of the Pharisees with His own more stringent interpretation of the Law.

Fourth, this view of the exception clause contradicts the teaching of Paul in 1 Corinthians 7:10-11 in which he claims to give the Lord's instruction and twice commands no separation. He exhorts married couples that the wife should not divorce (literally, "depart from") her husband, and that the husband should not divorce (literally, "send away") his wife. Paul, like Jesus in Mark and Luke, forbids divorce absolutely. The apostle claims to be giving Christ's own command for "no divorce," and does not mention any exceptions.

Finally, the word used in the exception clause (*porneia*) is not the normal word for adultery. The Greek word *moicheia* is the normal term used of adultery—sexual unfaithfulness to the marriage commitment. *Porneia*, on the other hand, is a much broader term which may include adultery, but refers to the other unlawful sexual behavior as well. The difference between these terms is evidenced by their use in several biblical passages to describe two different sins (cf. Matt. 15:19; Mark 7:22; 1 Cor. 6:9; Gal. 5:19; Heb. 13:4). The term Jesus uses in the exception clause is *porneia*—fornication. Why did He not use the word *moicheia*—adultery? Had Jesus intended to permit divorce in the case of adultery, He probably would have used *moicheia*, the more explicit term. The fact that He used another word indicates to me that His reference in the exceptive clause is something other than adultery.

2. *Unfaithfulness during the betrothal period.* Another interpretation of the exception clause is that Jesus permitted divorce and remarriage in the case of unfaithfulness during the betrothal period.[7] A little cultural background to marriage in New Testament times will be helpful at this point. The first step toward marriage in Jesus' day was the bridegroom's payment of a "bride price" or dowry to the father of the bride for the economic loss to the family. This would compensate the father of the bride for giving up a daughter who could tend his flocks, work in the fields, and carry water! Then a betrothal or promise of marriage was effected. Rings were exchanged and vows were spoken, but the marriage was not consummated. At least twelve months elapsed between betrothal and the actual wedding. During this period the bride would gather her wardrobe and prepare herself for married life. The bridegroom would prepare living accommodations in his father's house for his bride. She would be led in procession with her friends, family, and attendants by torchlight from her home to that of her husband's. There the marriage formula was pronounced and legal documents signed. Then during the wedding feast that followed, the bride and groom would slip into the bridal chamber and consummate the marriage by their physical union.[8]

Understand that Jewish betrothal, unlike modern engagement, was a legal contract which could be broken only by formal divorce or death.[9] Betrothal was as binding as marriage (cf. Deut. 20:7; 24:5)! If the betrothed proved unfaithful during the waiting period, or was discovered on the first night of marriage not to be a virgin, then a lawsuit could be filed and the partner divorced. Following this custom, Joseph was going to divorce Mary privately when she was discovered to be pregnant (Matt. 1:19). An angel then appeared to him in a dream and assured him that Mary had not been unfaithful, that the conception had taken place miraculously by the Holy Spirit!

According to this view of the exception clause, divorce could be permitted during the betrothal period, but once the marriage was consummated, then only death could break the union. The exception clause would have application only to the Jewish betrothal institution of ancient times and not to modern marriages. The application would be limited by the Jewish context and culture.

This view of the exception clause does take into consideration the Jewish context of Matthew's Gospel, and Matthew 1:19 does appear to illustrate such a practice and support this position. The most obvious objection to the betrothal thesis is that Jesus and the Pharisees were not discussing betrothal but *marriage*. The very passages which Jesus and the Pharisees referred to (Gen. 2:24; Deut. 24:1-4) speak of marriage relationships, not betrothal. In addition, this interpretation of *porneia* would not account for the absence of the exception in Mark and Luke, for both the Greeks and Romans, as well as the Jews, had such a betrothal period to which the exception would apply.[10] While it could be argued that the binding nature of betrothal among the Jews was unique, this does not adequately account for the presence of the exception clause in Matthew's Gospel alone. A more satisfactory explanation is possible.

3. *Unlawful marriage with Gentile idolaters*. A third possible interpretation of the exception clause of Matthew 5:32 and 19:9 is that *porneia* refers to unlawful marriage with Gentile idolaters.* Several occasions of such marriages and subsequent divorces are recorded in the Old Testament. Ezra required certain Jews to divorce their Gentile wives in order to keep the Jewish line pure and free from

---

*Coiner refers to this position in his survey, but does not support it, p. 375.

idolatry (Ezra 9-10). Later the prophet Malachi rebuked the Jews who had married idolatrous foreign women during Nehemiah's absence (Mal. 2:11). When governor Nehemiah returned to Jerusalem, he purged the Judeans of their relationships with the foreigners in order to keep the Jews from idolatry and apostasy (Neh. 13:23-31). Possibly Jesus was saying that a marriage contract could be annulled when a backslidden Jew married a Gentile; the purpose of the divorce being the preservation of the Jewish people and their faith.

This view of the exception clause would certainly account for its inclusion in the Jewish Gospel—Matthew. However, what took place in the restoration community under the leadership of Ezra and Nehemiah seems to have been a unique occurrence. The separation from the Gentile wives was necessary to insure the continued existence of the nation (cf. Deut. 7:3-4). The best argument against this view of the exception clause is an appeal to the writings of Paul. Since the Apostle Paul taught Jesus' view on divorce and remarriage and commanded the believing partner not to send the unbelieving partner away (1 Cor. 7:10, 12-13), we can be sure that Jesus was not teaching that one might divorce his or her unbelieving spouse. Scripture is its own best interpreter, and thus the clear teaching of Paul refutes the view that the exception clause allowed divorce in the case of the unlawful marriage of Jews to Gentile idolaters.

4. *Marriage within the prohibited relationships of Leviticus 18.* According to this view advocated by W. K. Lowther Clarke and more recently by Charles Ryrie,[11] the "except for *porneia*" would refer to marriage within the prohibited relationships of Leviticus 18:6-18. There in the context of God's demand for practical holiness among His people (Lev. 18-20), we find that marriage to a near relative is forbidden. The phrase used repeatedly, "to uncover the nakedness of," is a Hebrew euphemism for sexual inter-

course (cf. Deut. 22:30), and apparently refers here to marriage (Lev. 18:18). The unions condemned in Leviticus 18 would be the result of sexual passion rather than genuine love and affection. According to this interpretation of the exception clause, one who has married a near relative in violation of Jewish law should seek annulment, but for all others divorce is disallowed. Jesus, then, is basically teaching "no divorce," but one unique exception may be recognized when marriage has taken place within the prohibited degrees of Leviticus 18:6-18. It might be argued that the prohibition against incestuous marriage precludes any biblical provision for a legitimate divorce. But this objection does not hold up under close scrutiny, for the Israelites were commanded not to marry foreign women (Deut. 7:3-4), but when the command was violated in Ezra 9-10, the unlawful marriages were dissolved. The prohibition would not preclude the possibility of violation and the need to deal with an illegal incestuous situation.

This view of the exception clause in Matthew seems to me to be the most satisfactory position and has been recently commended for our consideration by the noted New Testament scholar, F. F. Bruce. Having examined other possible interpretations of *porneia* as used in Acts 15:20, 29, Bruce points out, "But fornication could bear a more technical sense of marital union within the prohibited degrees of consanguinity or affinity laid down by the Hebrew 'law of holiness' (Leviticus 18:6-18). There are one or two other places in the New Testament where fornication may have this technical sense—e.g. the concession 'except on the ground of fornication' added in the Matthaean version of Jesus' prohibition of divorce for his followers (Matthew 5:32, 19:9)."* This view of the exception clause can be supported by the following arguments:

---

*F. F. Bruce, *Paul: Apostle of the Heart Set Free* (Grand Rapids: Wm. B. Eerdmans Publishing Company, 1977), p. 185. Bruce definitely interprets Jesus as teaching the permanence of marriage and that divorce had no part in God's original plan (cf. pp. 59, 106).

a. *New Testament usage.* Since one possible lexical meaning of *porneia* is "incest" or "incestuous marriage,"[12] this interpretation must at least be considered as we seek to determine the meaning in a particular context. We find that this is the meaning of *porneia* in 1 Corinthians 5:1 which has reference to a man's marriage to his father's widow, a flagrant violation of Leviticus 18:8. Interpreting the exception clause to refer to incestuous marriage would also follow the meaning of *porneia* in Acts 15:20, 29 where certain practices are forbidden because of the offense to the Jews. In the letter sent to the churches by the Jerusalem Council, the apostles and elders instructed the Gentile believers to abstain from things sacrificed to idols, from blood, from things strangled, and from *porneia*. Note the order suggested first by James (Acts 15:20) and then given by the Council (Acts15:29):

James

Idol Sacrifices	Lev. 17:8-9
Porneia	Lev. 18:6-18
Things Strangled	Lev. 17:13-14
Blood	Lev. 17:10-12

The Council

Idol Sacrifices	Lev. 17:8-9
Blood	Lev. 17:10-12
Things Strangled	Lev. 17:13-14
Porneia	Lev. 18:6-18

It is quite apparent that James was thinking of the Leviticus 17-18 restrictions, but suggested them in the wrong order (Acts 15:20). Then, when the Council formulated its decision, the restrictions were recorded in their correct order according to Leviticus 17-18 (Acts 15:29).

While *porneia* can refer to every kind of unlawful sexual intercourse (cf. 1 Cor. 6:13; 2 Cor. 12:21; Gal. 5:19), context must always determine the specific meaning of a word. The immediate context of Acts 15:29 when compared with Leviticus 17-18 would indicate that it refers to the forbidden marriage relationships of Leviticus 18:6-18.*

There would have been no question about the illegitimacy of illicit sexual intercourse, condemned both by Jesus and Paul (Matt. 5:27-29; Gal. 5:19-21), but marriage within the prohibited relationships of Leviticus 18 was apparently a live issue (cf. 1 Cor. 5:1). The continuation of such a practice by Gentiles in the early church would obviously have been a grave offense to the Jews. Clearly, one possible meaning of *porneia* as used in the New Testament is that of incest or incestuous marriage. This meaning must at least be considered as a *possible* interpretation of *porneia* as found in Matthew 5:32 and 19:9.

b. *Jewish literature*. In addition to the New Testament evidence for this specialized use of the word *porneia*, Joseph Fitzmyer appeals to the Qumran materials to demonstrate that *porneia's* Hebrew counterpart, *zenut* (cf. LXX Jer. 3:2, 9), is used of marriage within the forbidden degrees of kinship.[13] There is, then, clear first-century Palestinian support for an interpretation of *porneia* in Matthew 5:32 and 19:9 as a specific reference to an illicit marital union between persons of close kinship. In later Judaism, the rabbis used *porneia* not only in a general sense to refer to every kind of extra-marital sexual intercourse, but also in the specialized sense of marriage between near relatives such as that forbidden by Leviticus 18:6-18.[14]

c. *Jewish context*. According to this interpretation, the matter of *porneia* would be a problem primarily for Jewish readers acquainted with the Old Testament Law, and would account for its inclusion in Matthew (to Jewish read-

---

*It is quite unlikely that the restrictions formulated by the Jerusalem Council included the sexual aberrations of Lev. 18:19-23. The matters of verses 19-23 are moral rather than ceremonial in nature and could not have been tolerated by either believing Jews or Gentiles. The concern of the Jerusalem Council was to address issues which might be considered "gray" areas—things which were acceptable to Gentiles but offensive to the Jews. The sins of Lev. 18:19-23 would have been condemned by both.

ers) and its absence in Mark and Luke (to Roman and Greek readers respectively). We must understand and appreciate the fact that each gospel writer was selective in what he chose to include in his record of Christ's life and teachings (cf. Luke 1:1-4; John 20:30; 21:25). While Mark was led by the Holy Spirit to record Jesus' teaching which applied the same rule of divorce and remarriage to both the husband and the *wife* (Mark 10:12), Matthew gives us no record of this teaching. Why? Because it was common in Roman and Greek society for a wife to divorce her husband, whereas Jewish law made no provision for this. Matthew, therefore, omitted this teaching because it did not apply to the Jewish culture and setting. On the other hand, Matthew does include the exception clause ("except for *porneia*"). He does this in view of the fact that he is writing to a Jewish audience familiar with the Leviticus 18:6-18 prohibition against marriage with a near relative. Mark apparently omits this because of its lack of application to Roman society and marriage customs. The Leviticus 18:6-18 interpretation of *porneia* would well explain the inclusion of the exception clause in Matthew—the Jewish Gospel—and its absence in Mark and Luke.

d. *Historical background*. Interpreting the exception clause of Matthew to refer to the Leviticus 18:6-18 prohibition against incestuous marriage would also fit well with the historical background of Jesus' confrontation with the Pharisees. As you recall, John the Baptist had been arrested, imprisoned, and eventually executed for speaking out against Herod Antipas who had divorced his wife and married his niece, the former wife of his brother Philip.[15] Recognizing this marriage to be in violation of Jewish Law, John declared to Herod Antipas, "It is not lawful for you to have her" (Matt. 14:4). Precisely what Jewish law had Herod Antipas violated? Leviticus 18:16 commands, "You shall not uncover the nakedness of your brother's wife; it is your brother's nakedness." Again in Leviticus 20:21, "If there is a man who takes his brother's wife, it is abhorrent; he has uncovered his brother's nakedness." John the Baptist condemned Herod Antipas not only for divorcing his wife, but also for marrying another woman in violation of Leviticus 18:16 and 20:21.

Since Jesus was being interrogated by the Pharisees in Perea (Matt. 19:1; Mark 10:1), the territory under the jurisdiction of Herod Antipas, it is quite likely that the Pharisees were trying to trick Jesus into making a statement against the marriage of Herod Antipas. They correctly assumed that since John and Jesus preached the same message (cf. Matt. 3:2; 4:17), they probably held the same views on marriage. Jesus followed John in condemning incestuous marriage, but while John declared directly, "It is not lawful," Jesus avoided a confrontation with Herod Antipas by simply stating that in the case of such an unlawful marriage, divorce was permitted. Thus, the historical background of John the Baptist's preaching and arrest points to *porneia* as being a reference to marriage within the near relationships prohibited by Leviticus 18:6-18.

e. *Immediate context.* One final argument for this specialized use of *porneia* in Matthew 5:32 and 19:9 is the immediate context in which the exception is found. If *porneia* refers to the prohibited relationships of Leviticus 18:6-18, then Jesus' teaching is consistent with God's ideal for marriage as set forth in Matthew 19:4-6 and Mark 10:6-8. God's plan for marriage does not include divorce except in the case of what the Jews would understand as an illegal marriage—a marriage relationship with a next of kin. In all other situations marriage is lifelong and binding until death!

This strict view of *porneia* would also explain the reaction of the disciples, "If the relationship of the man with his wife is like this, it is better not to marry" (Matt. 19:10). Had Jesus permitted divorce for adultery or other illicit sexual behavior, His teaching would not have risen above that of Shammai, and would not have provoked such a response.

Conclusion and Application

There is considerable support for the fourth view, that the exception clause permitted divorce when there had been an illegal marriage—a marriage within the prohibited relationships of Leviticus 18:6-18. While *porneia* can be used in a broad sense in the New Testament to refer to any kind of unlawful sexual activity, the Jewish setting, historical background, and immediate context of Matthew 19:1-12 have led me to conclude that Jesus was using the term in a specialized sense to refer to incestuous marriage. This view of *porneia* would be consistent with the teaching throughout Scripture that marriage is a lifelong relationship—permanent until death. I believe that the least tenable position is the first view, that Christ allowed divorce in the case of adultery. A clear understanding of *porneia* would indicate that He had something other than adultery in mind.

While some might argue that this is a rather "obscure" or even "esoteric" interpretation, I would hasten to say that it has both lexical and biblical support. It is a viable biblical alternative to the more lenient views and cannot be dismissed as "obscure" by serious students of God's Word. To some it may appear "obscure" because it is *different* from any view they have previously encountered. In teaching my Bible survey courses at the seminary I am regularly confronted with different views as I research problem passages. Sometimes I find a "different" view that is *better* than my own! Being different does not make an interpretation right or wrong. For those who seek the truth, each interpretation of the exception clause must be carefully and fairly considered as the evidence for each is weighed.

Now the question naturally arises, "How likely is it that a person would stumble into an incestuous marriage unknowingly?" The chances for such a mishap would be unlikely indeed. Herod Antipas married his niece, the former wife of his brother, knowingly and intentionally. Archelaus, who ruled Judea from 4 B.C. to A.D. 6, also entered into an incestuous marriage when he divorced his wife and married Glaphyra, the former wife of his half brother, Alexander.[16] Herod Agrippa II (A.D. 50-100) was reputedly involved in an incestuous relationship with his sister, Berniece.[17]

Incestuous marriage was obviously rather popular among the political leaders of Palestine in the first century, but these violations of levitical law were probably all committed out of lustful desire. None of these rulers stumbled into their incestuous relationships unknowingly. I do not believe that Jesus is opening up the spillways for divorce and remarriage with the *porneia* exception. Rather, the point Jesus seems to be making in Matthew 19:9 is that it would be better for a couple to separate and end an illegal marriage than to continue an illicit sexual relationship. Jesus may well have had Herod Antipas in mind, but the teaching would apply as well to others in the same situation.

Today people debate, "Is it right for divorced people to remarry?" Christ dealt with the issue, "Is it right for married people to be divorced?" Note the contrast! The answer Jesus gives is, "Absolutely not!" The clear teaching of Jesus concerning divorce and remarriage as recorded in the Synoptic Gospels is that the God-ordained marriage union is indissoluble, and that divorce and remarriage is adultery.

Jesus' teaching on divorce and remarriage is quite strict in contrast with the ways of modern society and even the ways of the evangelical church. Though we may not understand completely the sacredness and inviolability of the marriage union that God demands we preserve, the believer is responsible to obey the teaching of Jesus because of love for Him: "If you love Me, you will keep My commandments" (John 14:15).

Study Questions

1. What evidence is there that Matthew gives us a unique Jewish gospel? How does this seem to explain why he includes some data while omitting other material?
2. What significant contributions does Matthew's Gospel make in recording Jesus' teaching on divorce and remarriage?
3. Jesus allows divorce for one cause—*porneia*. Why is it probable that this Greek word does not refer to adultery in the context of Matthew 19?
4. If Jesus had argued that divorce was permitted in the case of adultery, how could He have made himself more clear?
5. Explain the betrothal custom of biblical times. Could *porneia* possibly have reference to unfaithfulness during the betrothal period? What are the pros and cons?
6. Could *porneia* possibly refer to unlawful marriage with Gentile idolaters? Why or why not?
7. Leviticus 18:6-18 prohibits marriage between near relatives. What New Testament evidence is there that the *porneia* of Matthew 5:32 and 19:9 might have reference to such illegal marriage relationships?
8. How does the historical background of John the Baptist's ministry help in determining the meaning of *porneia* in Matthew 5:32 and 19:9?

Notes

1. Eusebius *Historia Ecclesiastica* 2.15.
2. Josephus *Antiquities* XV. 259.
3. W. T. Manson, *The Teachings of Jesus* (Cambridge: University Press, 1951), p. 200.

4. *Theological Dictionary of the New Testament*, eds. Gerhard Kittel and Gerhard Friedrich, trans. and ed. Geoffrey W. Bromiley, s.v. *Porne, Pornos, Porneia, Porneuo, Ekporneuō*, by Hauck/Schulz, 6 (1968), p. 580.

5. *A Greek-English Lexicon of the New Testament and Other Early Christian Literature*, trans. William F. Arndt and F. Wilbur Gingrich, 1957 ed., s.v. *Porneia*, pp. 669-70.

6. John Murray, *Divorce* (Philadelphia: Orthodox Presbyterian Church, 1953), pp. 47-48; Loraine Boettner, *Divorce* (Nutley, New Jersey: Presbyterian and Reformed Publishing Co., 1974), pp. 11-21.

7. James Montgomery Boice, "The Biblical View of Divorce," *Eternity* 21 (December 1970), p. 20; Abel Isaksson, *Marriage and Ministry in the New Temple* (Lund: C.W.K. Gleerup, 1965), pp. 75-92.

8. Fred H. Wight, *Manners and Customs of Bible Lands* (Chicago: Moody Press, 1953), pp. 124-34.

9. Alfred Edersheim, *The Life and Times of Jesus the Messiah*, one vol. ed. (Grand Rapids: Wm. B. Eerdman's Publishing Company, 1971), vol. i, p. 354.

10. *The Oxford Classical Dictionary*, eds. N.G.L. Hammond and H. H. Scullard, 2nd ed., s.v. "Betrothal, Greek," and "Betrothal, Roman," p. 166.

11. W. K. Lowther Clarke, "The Exceptive Clause in St. Matthew," *Theology* 15 (1927), pp. 161-62, and *New Testament Problems* (New York: Macmillan, 1929), pp. 59-6060; Charles C. Ryrie, *The Role of Women in the Church* (Chicago: Moody Press, 1970), pp. 40-50, and *You Mean the Bible Teaches That* (Chicago: Moody Press, 1974), pp. 45-46.

12. *Greek and English Lexicon of the New Testament*, ed. Edward Robinson, new and revised ed., s.v. *Porneia*, p.609.

13. Joseph A. Fitzmyer, "The Matthean Divorce Texts and Some New Palestinian Evidence," *Theological Studies* 37 (1976), pp. 213-21.

14. *Testament of Judah* 13:6; *Testament of Reuben* 1:6.
15. Josephus *Antiquities* XVIII. 109-119.]
16. Josephus *Wars* II. 114-116.
17. Josephus *Antiquities* XX. 145-147.

7

The Teaching of Paul

Robert is a mature Christian businessman, and until recently has been active as a leader in his local church. He and his wife, Sherry, were happily married for twenty-three years, and together raised two fine children. Through their years of marriage, they had together overcome several serious problems—Sherry's long bout with cancer and Bob's business indebtedness. Yet, by God's grace, they overcame these difficulties. Sherry's cancer went into remission, and Robert's business became financially stable and productive. With their two children "out of the nest," it would appear that this couple would be ready to sit back and begin to enjoy the "good life" together.

Then it happened! Without any warning or previous problems, Sherry told Robert she didn't love him anymore and wanted a divorce. Soon afterward, Sherry moved away and began living with another man. Robert was devastated! It took him over a year just to recover from the initial shock of the divorce and to begin to put the pieces of his life back together. Then he began asking, "What should I do?" He didn't enjoy living alone and wanted the companionship of a wife. Some would argue on the basis of 1 Corinthians 7:15 that Paul allows for divorce and remarriage not only in the case of adultery, but also in the case of abandonment. Does Robert have a right to remarry? What did Paul teach on the subject of divorce and remarriage?

In Romans 7:2-3:

> *For the married woman is bound by law to her husband while he is living; but if her husband dies, she is released from the law concerning the husband. So then if, while her husband is living, she is joined to another man, she shall be called an adulteress; but if her husband dies, she is free from the law, so that she is not an adulteress, though she is joined to another man.*

The New Testament teaching concerning divorce and remarriage is rounded out by the instruction of the Apostle Paul recorded in Romans and 1 Corinthians. Following the teaching of Jesus, Paul affirms that the marriage union is lifelong and indissoluble.

In Romans 7:1-6 Paul develops the concept of the believer's release from the law, a theme first introduced in Romans 6:14, "For sin shall not be master over you, for you are not under law, but under grace."[1] In Romans 7:1-3 Paul sets forth a principle, and then an illustration. The principle stated in verse 1 is simply that death ends the dominion of the law. The jurisdiction of the law is limited to *living* individuals! Death releases one from further obligation to the Mosaic code. Paul proceeds in verses 2 and 3 to illustrate the principle of verse 1 from the relationship of marriage. Now his main concern in this context is the believer's release from the law, but his illustration sheds considerable light on the permanence of the marriage union.

Paul observes in verse 2 that a woman is bound to her husband as long as he lives (no exceptions!), but when he dies she is released from the marital relationship they enjoyed as husband and wife. Death and death alone affords release from the bond of marriage. Paul then notes in verse 3 that a woman who is "joined" to another man while her husband yet lives is an adulteress. The word "joined" refers not to illicit sexual relations, but to legal *marriage* as the last clause of verse 3 indicates, ". . . if her husband dies, . . . she is not an adulteress, though she is *joined* [i.e., married] to another man." Paul then applies the principle he has just illustrated by instructing the Roman readers that as believers they have died to the law and are joined to a new Master—Christ (Rom. 7:4-6). Those who are in Christ are no longer slaves to the law of sin and death. The believer who has died with Christ is released from bondage and is free to experience new and abundant life with Christ!

While Romans 7:1-6 is primarily concerned with the believer's release from the law, Paul's illustration from the marriage union sheds light on his view that marriage is permanent until death. Only death can break the marriage bond and release a spouse to marry another partner. This exact teaching is presented by Paul in 1 Corinthians 7:39 where he declares, "A wife is bound as long as her husband lives" (no exceptions)! Only when her husband dies is she free to be remarried. A second marriage while one's spouse yet lives, says Paul, is adultery.

In First Corinthians 7:10-16:

> But to the married I give instructions, not I, but the Lord, that the wife should not leave her husband (but if she does leave, let her remain unmarried, or else be reconciled to her husband), and that the husband should not send his wife away. But to the rest I say, not the Lord, that if any brother has a wife who is an unbeliever, and she consents to live with him, let him not send her away. And a woman who has an unbelieving husband, and he consents to live with her, let her not send her husband away. For the unbelieving husband is sanctified through his wife, and the unbelieving wife is sanctified through her believing husband; for otherwise your children are unclean, but now they are holy. Yet if the unbelieving one leaves, let him leave; the brother or the sister is not under bondage in such cases, but God has called us to peace. For how do you know, O wife, whether you will save your husband? Or how do you know, O husband, whether you will save your wife?

In this passage Paul replies to a number of inquiries made by the Corinthian believers. The key to this section is the repeated use of the introductory phrase "now concerning" (7:1; 8:1; 12:1; 16:1). In chapter 7 Paul responds to several questions concerning marriage which the Corinthian believers were asking. He begins the chapter by stating some general principles about marriage. While Paul permits marriage, he prefers the single life (7:1, 2, 7). He does, however, encourage marriage for the unmarried men and widows who do not have the special gift of celibacy which includes total sexual self-control (7:8-9).

Next, Paul speaks to the married believers about maintaining their marriage relationships. Appealing to the teaching of Christ (cf. Mark 10:9, 11, 12; Luke 16:18), Paul declares in no uncertain terms that married persons should not seek divorce (7:10-11). Twice he affirms the principle of no divorce, ". . . the wife should not leave her husband" (7:10), and ". . . the husband should not send his wife away" (7:11). But what course of action should be followed when a divorce takes place anyway as in the case of Robert and Sherry? Paul gives us the answer in the form of a parenthesis in verse 11. If a divorce or separation should happen to take place, Paul leaves the believers with two options: (1) remain permanently unmarried—the present tense of "remain" emphasizing the permanent condition, or (2) be reconciled to one's partner—the aorist tense emphasizing the attainment of the end of the reconciliation process.[2] Since the culminative aorist is used here to regard the reconciliation from the viewpoint of its existing results,[3] no future separations are in view or contemplated.

Two crucial observations must be made at this point. First, Paul is not adding to the counsel of God in 1 Corinthians 7:10-11 but merely following the teaching of Jesus. On this matter, F. F. Bruce comments: "For a Christian husband or wife divorce is excluded by the law of Christ: here Paul has no need to express a judgment of his own, for the Lord's ruling on this matter was explicit."[4] Paul taught what Jesus taught on divorce and remarriage.

Second, Paul gives no exceptions to the principle of "no

divorce." In light of the clear teaching of the Apostle Paul, the only counsel we could give Robert is to remain permanently in an unmarried state, or to be reconciled to Sherry. The possibility of remarriage is simply not offered as a viable option. As Jesus says, to remarry would be to commit adultery (Luke 16:18).

In verses 12-16 Paul deals with the case where one partner becomes a believer after marriage. While Christ did not give any teaching concerning spiritually mixed marriages ("I say, not the Lord"), Paul does, and his teaching is divinely inspired and authoritative. Again Paul's instruction is *no separation* (7:12-13). He commands the believing husband not to send his wife away, and the believing wife not to send her husband away. The principle of "no divorce" is set forth four times in verses 10-13. Count them! A Christian, says Paul, should continue to live with the unbelieving partner as long as the unbelieving spouse consents to the arrangement. Three reasons for preserving the marriage union with the unbelieving partner are given: (1) for the sake of the family, v. 14; (2) for the sake of peace, v. 15; and (3) for the sake of personal testimony, v. 16. The presence of a believer in the home sets it apart ("sanctifies") and gives it a Christian influence it would not otherwise have. The testimony of the believer may be used by God to bring the children and unbelieving partner to Christ!

There are those who interpret verse 15 as an encouragement for separation or divorce in the interest of preserving peace, but the context certainly argues against this view (7:10-11, 16). Paul is simply saying that if an unbelieving partner demands separation, the believer is not "under bondage" (literally, "enslaved") to preserve the marriage union. Paul is saying that it is not necessary for the believer to contest the divorce action or engage in legal maneuvers to prevent it. Since God has called us to peace, the bitterness and strife of contesting a divorce or separation must be avoided. Notice, however, that Paul says nothing in verse

15 about a second marriage for the deserted spouse. In arguing the right of a deserted believer to remarry, one writer states, "If they could not remarry, they certainly were in bondage, were they not?"[5] But how can we advocate the possibility of a second marriage when Paul himself is silent! A key interpretive principle comes to our aid here. "Never allow a questionable or obscure interpretation to contradict the clear and positive teaching of Scripture." Applying this rule to 1 Corinthians 7:15 and its context, we can hardly conclude that Paul is teaching that divorce and remarriage in the case of desertion is not adultery.

If an unbelieving husband divorces his wife, she is no longer bound to her husband, but she is still bound to the law of God. The freedom of a deserted believer does not imply the freedom to marry.[6] The two alternatives of reconciliation or a lifelong single life would still apply (7:11). To interpret otherwise would be to contradict Paul's own words (Rom. 7:2-3; 1 Cor. 7:39) and the teaching of Jesus as well (Mark 10:11-12; Luke 16:18).

One other passage used by some to advocate remarriage for divorced persons is 1 Corinthians 7:27-28, "Are you released from a wife? Do not seek a wife. But if you should marry, you have not sinned." The context, of course, is the key to understanding this teaching. Paul is responding to a question concerning young unmarried women (7:25). His main point is that celibacy is desired, though not demanded (7:25-26). Paul proceeds to give three arguments for the single life. First, in light of the pressure on a Christian in an unfriendly world, it may not be wise to enter into marriage—its responsibilities would impose more pressure and burdens on the believer (7:26-28). The "present distress" (v. 26) may refer to some unique difficulties which the Corinthians were experiencing. The transitory nature of things in light of the Lord's return is the second argument given by Paul for remaining unmarried (7:29-31). Marriage and other such commitments must be viewed in light of the nearness of Christ's return. Paul's third argument for remaining unmarried is that it frees a believer for undistracted devotion and service for Christ (7:23-25).

Paul emphasizes for his readers that to marry is not to commit sin (7:28), but to incur greater responsibility and potential trouble in life. Therefore, he says, it is best to stay in the marital state you find yourself in. In light of this context we understand verse 27 to mean that one who has entered into marriage should not seek "release," nor should the unmarried seek marriage. In other words, remain married if you are married; single, if you are single.

The second question Paul asks in verse 27, "Are you released from a wife?" needs further comment. The perfect tense of the verb "released" refers not to freedom from marriage by the divorce of a spouse, but rather a state of freedom from matrimonial ties.[7] Paul is addressing his comments in verses 25-35 to unmarried persons—precisely virgins (7:25). His teaching here would, of course, apply as well to widows and widowers (cf. 7:39). Paul's main point set forth in verse 25 is the principle of marital status quo. Whether you are married or single, the Apostle Paul says stay that way! To argue that Paul is advocating the remarriage of divorced persons, and that this may be done without sin, is to violate the context of the passage and contradict the clear teaching of Paul elsewhere, and the teaching of Jesus in the gospels.

Summary and Conclusion

Like Jesus, the Apostle Paul affirms the principle of "no divorce." The marriage union is binding until death (Rom. 7:2-3; 1 Cor. 7:39). Under no circumstances—adultery or abandonment—should a believer seek a divorce. Paul says this four times in 1 Corinthians 7:10-13. If a divorce should take place in disregard of this instruction or prior to an understanding of it, Paul presents only two alternatives for the divorcée: reconciliation to one's spouse, or a lifelong single life. Paul taught a very strict position on divorce and re-marriage, but then so did Jesus. Both recognized that God's plan for marriage was a union that was binding and per-manent for life.

If Robert asked an unbeliever what he should do about his separation from Sherry, the advice he would probably receive would be to forget her and find a good woman to en-joy for the rest of his life. But if he asked Paul what he should do, Paul would say, "Be reconciled to Sherry or re-main unmarried." Since Robert does not want to live a sin-gle life, his prayers should be for reconciliation. But how can Robert love again his adulterous and unfaithful wife? How can he be reconciled to someone who has hurt him so? As Jesus said in Matthew 19:26, "With men this is impossi-ble, but with God all things are possible." The world recom-mends divorce when one's own meager resources of love and forgiveness are exhausted. But God delights in restoring marriages and thus proving to a skeptical world the reality and power of His love!

Study Questions

1. What major idea is Paul developing in Romans 7:1-6? How does the subject of marriage happen to fit in?
2. What light does Paul's illustration from the marriage union (Rom. 7:2-3) shed on his views concerning di-vorce and remarriage?
3. Where else in Paul's writings is the same truth of Ro-mans 7:2-3 confirmed?
4. In 1 Corinthians 7:10-11, Paul twice affirms the prin-ciple of "no divorce." What counsel does he give in the case where a divorce has already occurred?
5. What about the case of a believer married to an unbeliever? Is divorce an option in this situation?
6. What reasons does Paul give for preserving the mar-

riage union with an unbelieving partner (1 Cor. 7:14-16)?

7. Does 1 Corinthians 7:15 teach that divorce and remarriage is permitted in the case of desertion? What key interpretive principle helps us understand this verse?

8. Explain how 1 Corinthians 7:27 fits into the context of 7:25-35. Is Paul implying in verse 27 that some divorced persons may remarry without sin? Why or why not?

9. In light of Paul's definitive statements against divorce and remarriage, how would you counsel and encourage a divorced person who does not want to live a single life?

Notes

1. James M. Stifler, *The Epistle to the Romans* (Chicago: Moody Press, 1960), p. 118.

2. S. Lewis Johnson, "First Corinthians" in *The Wycliffe Bible Commentary*, eds. Charles F. Pfeiffer and Everett F. Harrison (Chicago: Moody Press), p. 1240.

3. H. E. Dana and Julius R. Mantey, *A Manual Grammar of the Greek New Testament* (Toronto, Ontario: The Macmillan Company, 1927), p. 196.

4. F. F Bruce, *Paul: Apostle of the Heart Set Free* (Grand Rapids: Wm. B. Eerdmans Publishing Company, 1977), p. 267.

5. Guy Duty, *Divorce and Remarriage* (Minneapolis, Minnesota: Bethany Fellowship, Inc., 1967), p. 100.

6. W. Fisher-Hunter, *Marriage and Divorce: A Biblical Treatise on Divorce* (Waynesboro, Pennsylvania: MacNeish Publishers, 1952), p. 109.

7. A. T. Robertson and Alfred Plummer, *The First Epistle of St. Paul to the Corinthians*, 2nd ed., *The International Critical Commentary* (Edinburgh: T. & T. Clark, 1911), p. 153.

8

Divorce and the Christian Ministry

The Admissions Committee at the seminary where I teach recently received a letter from a young man, whom we'll call Brian, who was considering applying for our Master of Divinity program. He had written to ask if his marital situation would disqualify him from admission to the program, which is designed to prepare men for the pastorate. In a very candid manner he related that he had become a Christian as a young person, and at an early age sensed the Lord's call to Christian service. Brian began to grow in Christ, but then for some undisclosed reason stopped walking with the Lord. During that time away from the Lord, Brian began dating a divorcée. They yielded to sexual temptation, and consequently the woman became pregnant.

Following the counsel of a pastor friend, Brian married the woman and they now have a happy marriage. Brian is now in fellowship with God and believes he should honor his earlier "call" to serve the Lord. In order to prepare for Christian service, he desires seminary training. Brian admits that he sinned against God but recognizes that he is completely forgiven. He writes, "There is nothing that I know of in the Bible that would disqualify me from Christian service."

This letter raises a most significant issue in our consideration of what the Bible has to say about divorce and remarriage. Is a divorced man biblically qualified to be a pastor/elder? How about the situation of Brian who has married a divorcée? Does marrying a divorcée disqualify one from Christian ministry? Does the same standard of marital status apply to both the pastor/elder and deacon? If a divorced person is not biblically qualified to be a pastor or elder, how can he exercise his spiritual gifts? What *can* he do to serve Christ? Let's turn Brian's statement into a question and discover together, "Is there anything in the Bible that would disqualify a divorced person from Christian ministry?"

The Old Testament Precedent

> *They [the priests] shall not take a woman who is profaned by harlotry, nor shall they take a woman divorced from her husband; for he is holy to his God. (Lev. 21:7)*

> *A widow, or a divorced woman, or one who is profaned by harlotry, these he [the high priest] may not take; but rather he is to marry a virgin of his own people; that he may not profane his offspring among his people; for I am the Lord who sanctifies him. (Lev. 21:14-15)*

The holiness of the Lord and the resultant holiness of His chosen people is the central theme of Leviticus (cf. Lev. 20:26). Since God is holy, those who are His ought to be separated from the world unto the service and glory of God. Now if the people are to be separated from everything evil, how much more ought the priests who present the offerings and sacrifices to the Lord! Leviticus 21-22 legislates matters of holiness in priestly conduct and duties, showing that God appointed a higher standard of holiness for the priests than for the rest of the people of Israel. This is especially seen in the regulations concerning death and marriage.

According to the Bible, death is the penalty for sin (Gen. 2:17; 3:19; Rom. 5:12; 6:23), and thus is ceremonially defiling. One who touched a corpse in the Old Testament period would be "unclean" for seven days (Num. 19:11).

God did provide the cleansing of the people through the red-heifer ordinance (Num. 19:1-10). Interestingly, God prohibited the priests from having contact with the dead except in the case of close relatives (Lev. 21:1-3). In the case of the high priest, he was to avoid the defilement of death and mourning without any exceptions (Lev. 21:10-12)! We find here that God has a higher standard of holiness for His priests than for the people. The same is true in the matter of marriage.

According to Mosaic law, the priests were not to marry a woman defiled by harlotry or divorced from her husband (Lev. 21:7). To do so would bring defilement to the priesthood! Similarly, the high priest was not to marry a widow, a divorced woman, or a woman defiled by harlotry (Lev. 21:14). He was required by law to marry a virgin of his own people lest his offspring be unfit for his holy office (Lev. 21:15). While no such restrictions or prohibitions are set forth for the lay people of Israel, the priests were to be beyond reproach in their marital relationships. During the Restoration Period Nehemiah took steps to expel the son of Eliashib, the high priest, from the priesthood because of his violation of levitical marriage laws (Neh. 13:27-29; Lev. 21:6-8, 14-15).

Both in the matter of the defilement of death and the requirements for marriage, God has higher standards for the spiritual leaders of His people than for those who are being led. This is illustrated as well in the requirement that the priests totally abstain from the use of alcoholic beverages when officiating in the tabernacle (Lev. 10:9; cf. Ezek. 44:21). Notice as well the words of King Lemuel in Proverbs 31:4-5, "It is not for kings . . . to drink wine, or for rulers to desire strong drink, lest they drink and forget what is decreed, and pervert the right of all the afflicted." Not all qualify to lead God's people!

The Old Testament sets the precedent in requiring that the priests, the spiritual leaders of the people, be above reproach in their marital situation. This principle of high marriage standards for spiritual leaders in the Old Testament corresponds well with the marriage qualifications set forth by Paul for the New Testament elders and deacons.

The New Testament Requirement

An overseer, then, must be above reproach, the husband of one wife. (1 Tim. 3:2)

Let deacons be husbands of only one wife, and good managers of their children and their own households. (1 Tim. 3:12)

Namely, if any man be above reproach, the husband of one wife. . . . (Titus 1:6)

In 1 Timothy 3:1-13 and Titus 1:5-9 Paul sets forth the qualifications for the biblical church offices of elder (or overseer) and deacon. In 1 Timothy 3:1 Paul refers to the office of "overseer" while in giving the same qualifications for church leaders in Titus 1:5 he refers to the office of elder. A close examination of Acts 20:17, 28 will reveal that the two terms are used synonymously of the officially recognized spiritual leaders of the church. While the term "overseer" emphasizes the function of the office—oversight—the term "elder" emphasizes the dignity and maturity of the office. It is interesting that the title used most commonly in our churches today, namely "pastor," was not used in conjunction with the church in the New Testament. The term used for the gifted man, not office, in Ephesians 4:11 is literally, "shepherd," and the *chief* shepherd is Christ (1 Pet. 5:4). The office of elder involves oversight of members of a local congregation and involves shepherding (Acts 20:28; 1 Pet. 5:2), protecting (Acts 20:19-31), ruling (1 Tim. 5:17), teaching (1 Tim. 3:2; Titus 1:9), and ministering to the sick and suffering (James 1:27; 5:14-15).

It is important to realize that in 1 Timothy 3:1-13 and Titus 1:5-9, Paul is setting forth qualifications for office, not simply goals or objectives for which those in office are to strive. This is clear from Paul's statements, "An overseer, then, *must be*. . . " (1 Tim. 3:2, 7). The conditional phrase ("if . . . ") in Titus 1:6 implies that only those who meet the standards should be considered for appointment to the office. These verses, then, do not contain "qualitative guidelines" but rather minimal standards. These basic qualifications for the office of elder are designed to enable Timothy in Ephesus and Titus on Crete to appoint spiritual leadership of God's people. Not all men meet the standards, and while God can use men in other areas of Christian service, they are not biblically qualified for the office of elder or deacon.

The first qualification given by Paul is that the elder must be "above reproach"—blameless in his Christian character with no area of his life subject to criticism or vulnerable to attack. Then, Paul instructs that the elder must be the "husband of one wife" (1 Tim. 3:2; 3:12; Titus 1:6). This short phrase has been interpreted in many different ways and has been the subject of considerable discussion.[1] In the Greek text this expression is found without the article and thus it has a qualitative emphasis.[2] It could well be rendered "a one-woman man." What precisely does this qualification for the office of elder and deacon mean?

1. *Exclusion of married men.* In attempting to defend the Roman doctrine of celibacy for priests, some Catholics have argued that this means the priest is to be married to one wife—the Church. This view, however, is refuted right in the context where we read that the elder is one "keeping his children under control" (3:4). Also in 1 Timothy 4:3 Paul says that forbidding marriage is one of the doctrines of false teachers. Marriage is a God-ordained and honorable state (Gen. 2:24; Heb. 13:4). In all fairness to Catholic scholars, it must be said that this view is not widely held. It is almost universally recognized that priestly celibacy was an ecclesiastical law enacted later in the history of the church.[3]

2. *Exclusion of unmarried men*. Another interpretation of the "husband of one wife" qualification is that it excludes unmarried men from the office of overseer or deacon. However, Paul saw nothing wrong with the single state and even encouraged it (1 Cor. 7:7, 8, 17). In fact, Paul himself was an elder (compare 1 Tim. 4:14 with 2 Tim. 1:6) and yet was unmarried (1 Cor. 7:8)! Consistency of interpretation would mean that if the elder must be married, he must also have children (1 Tim. 3:4), and yet no expositor that I am aware of is willing to push the issue that far.

3. *Exclusion of polygamists*. Others, such as John Calvin, have understood the phrase "husband of one wife" to prohibit polygamy for church leaders.[4] However, in the time during which Paul was writing, polygamy was forbidden in the empire by Roman law.[5] Polygamy was not practiced by the Greeks or the Romans of the New Testament period. An additional argument against this view is that there would be no need for this qualification in light of the fact that Paul forbad such immorality for all believers, not just the church leaders (1 Cor. 7:2).

4. *Exclusion of digamists*. The fourth major interpretation of the marital qualification of elder and deacon is that it forbids digamy—being married twice (or more) legally. According to this view divorce and remarriage, though according to civil law, would disqualify a man from the office of elder or deacon. Some have argued that Paul allowed for divorced overseers and have interpreted the phrase to mean "one wife at a time." But to include such a qualification would be absurd since virtually anyone could meet the standard. The view that the marital qualification for elder is being devoted to "one wife at a time" is also refuted by the requirement that the elder or deacon be one who "manages his own household well" (1 Tim. 3:4,12). The disaster of divorce and remarriage would be evidence of the mismanagement of one's household.

I would suggest that divorce and remarriage or marital infidelity, whether before or after conversion, would disqualify one from the office of elder or deacon. The prohibition given the sons of Aaron against marrying a divorced woman (Lev. 21:7, 14) would confirm the teaching of the New Testament that there are higher marriage standards for elders and deacons. The anarthrous (without the definite article) construction of the phrase would emphasize the quality or character of the individual as a "one wife husband." Most fundamentally, this would refer to one marriage—no divorce. The "one" is in a place of emphasis and contrasts with the idea of "many." Beyond that, the qualification would refer to a man totally devoted to one woman—no infidelity. It would also mean a man who was not lusting after other women (Matt. 5:28)—no wandering eyeballs.

In addition, some believe that the qualification "husband of one wife" would exclude remarried widowers from church office. This view was commonly held by the church fathers. According to this view, the marital qualification of 1 Timothy 3 demands that the elder or deacon be married just *once*. This may be inferred from the requirement that widows receiving church support be the "wife of one man" (1 Tim. 5:9). The phrase corresponds to our "husband of one wife" and in this context may indicate being married just once. Since the widows on the list must not have been married a second time, this qualification would correspond to that of the elder.

The primary objection to this view is that it *seems* to presuppose that marriage is almost a necessary evil, and that while one marriage is permitted, a second marriage would be a sign of moral weakness. Such a view of marriage is clearly out of harmony with Scripture. The Bible reveals that marriage is a good and honorable estate. However, rather than reflecting a low view of marriage, this qualification could presuppose that the elder or deacon is a Christian characterized by total commitment to Christ and His church (cf. 1 Cor. 7:32-34). A second marriage and family responsibilities could certainly limit a believer's opportunity for Christian ministry. One who prefers a second marriage over greater opportunities for service to Christ may not be biblically qualified to serve in the office of elder or deacon.

Another objection to this view is that Paul said elsewhere that remarriage was permitted after the death of a spouse (1 Cor. 7:39 and 1 Tim. 5:14). However, there is no contradiction here, for the prohibition in 1 Timothy 3 is in relationship to the elders and deacons, while the words in 1 Corinthians 7:39 and 1 Timothy 5:14 are addressed to widows.[6] Such restrictions against a second marriage would apply only to elders and deacons of the church whose leadership responsibilities may somewhat restrict their personal liberty in the area of marriage.

Some might argue that the qualification "husband of one wife" means that it is not the divorce *per se*, but remarriage which would disqualify one from the office of elder or deacon. Thus a divorced believer preparing for the pastoral ministry could possibly meet the qualifications for the office of elder by remaining single. There are at least three major objections to such a view. First, the elder and deacon must be above reproach (1 Tim. 3:2, 10)—blameless! Although the circumstances vary, it generally takes *two* to make a divorce. A divorced man, though remaining single, would probably not be "above reproach." Second, the elder and deacon must be men who manage their household well (1 Tim. 3:4-5, 12). Divorce would certainly be an evidence of one's mismanagement of his household. Third, with reference to the deacons, Paul says, "Women must likewise be dignified, not malicious gossips, but temperate, faithful in all things" (1 Tim. 3:11). There is some debate as to whether this verse refers to deacons wives or deaconesses. I, however, find reason to doubt that there was an office of "deaconess" in the early church.* This verse seems to indicate that the wives of the spiritual leaders of the church must be exemplary in their conduct and *faithful in all things*. Thus a wife who is unfaithful to her marriage vow would disqualify her husband from a position in church leadership. It is remarkable what a positive or negative effect a wife can have on one's ministry!

Conclusion and Application

A study of both the Old Testament and New Testament reveals that God has high marital qualifications for the spiritual leaders of His people. The principle of high marriage standards for the Old Testament priests (Lev. 21:7, 14-15) corresponds well with the marriage qualifications set forth by Paul for the New Testament elder and deacon (1 Tim. 3:2, 12; Titus 1:6). The elder and deacon of the New Testament church must be the "husband of one wife"— married just once. One who is divorced and remarried would be disqualified, and possibly also the remarried widower. The requirement would also disqualify one who is not totally devoted to his one wife and in the habit of lusting after other women. Admittedly, the standard is high, but should God and the Christian Church expect less of those who will be giving spiritual leadership to the body of Christ?

What about the case of Brian who married a divorced woman and yet wants to train for the Christian ministry? What counsel and direction could we give him? While he would appear to meet the qualification "Husband of one wife," he certainly would not be "above reproach." Jesus

---

*See Charles Caldwell Ryrie, *The Role of Women in the Church* (Chicago: Moody Press, 1958), pp. 85-91. Phoebe is called a deacon—literally "servant"—in Romans 16:1, but this is probably an unofficial use of the word as in Colossians 1:7.

says in Luke 16:18, "Everyone who divorces his wife and marries another commits adultery; and he who marries one who is divorced from a husband commits adultery." Since the God-ordained marriage union is lifelong, to marry a divorced person would be to enter into an existing marriage and hence, to commit adultery. Brian, then, according to the clear teaching of the Bible would not be biblically qualified.

I once held the view that while divorce and remarriage would disqualify one from the *office* of elder or deacon, it would be acceptable for a divorced person to *function* in such capacities unofficially. In other words, a divorced person could not be an elder, but he could be a church planter or teach in a church or seminary setting. I have been challenged on this view on several occasions and must now concede that my emphasis was on the "letter of the law" rather than the "spirit" of the New Testament teaching. Certainly God intends for His high marriage standards for church leaders to apply both to officially recognized elders and deacons *and* to those who do the work of an elder in an unofficial capacity. For example, while I am not an elder in a local church, I function as a teaching elder with oversight over young men and women at seminary. I am now convinced that there is little difference between "office" and "function" in the context of the qualifications for elders and deacons. While *functioning* as an elder, God's marriage standards for elders would apply to me as well.

I do believe there are opportunities for Christian service that could be pursued by a divorced or divorced and remarried person—evangelism, discipleship, counseling, and many other support ministries serving the local church and missionary groups. I would encourage Brian to plan to serve Christ in some capacity other than that of elder or deacon. Divorce and remarriage does limit the extent of one's Christian service, but does not disqualify a Christian from service to the body of Christ altogether! There are abundant opportunities for a Christian to exercise his spiritual gifts apart from serving in the *office* or *functioning* as a deacon or elder.

Study Questions

1. According to the Old Testament Law, who was a priest prohibited from marrying?
2. What light does the Old Testament shed on God's standards for the spiritual leaders of His people?
3. What evidence is there that the terms "elder" and "overseer" are used of the same church office? What does each term emphasize?
4. Are the characteristics set forth in 1 Timothy 3:1-13 and Titus 1:5-9 qualifications for office, or objectives for which those in office are to strive? Why?
5. Briefly summarize the four main interpretations of the phrase "husband of one wife." Why is it unlikely that Paul meant for the qualification to exclude polygamists from church office?
6. What is "digamy"? Why is it highly unlikely that Paul would have allowed a divorced man to be appointed to the office of elder or deacon?
7. Would the qualification "husband of one wife" exclude remarried widowers from church office? Why or why not?
8. Would a divorced man who had not remarried meet the biblical qualifications for church office? Explain your answer.

Notes

1. Homer A. Kent, *The Pastoral Epistles* (Chicago: Moody Press, 1958), pp. 126-30; Robert L. Saucy, "The

Husband of One Wife," *Bibliotheca Sacra* 131 (July-September 1974), pp. 229-40.

2. H. E. Dana and J. R. Mantey, *A Manual Grammar of the Greek New Testament* (Toronto: The Macmillan Company, 1927), pp. 149-50.

3. *New Catholic Encyclopedia*, s.v. "Celibacy," by P. Delhaye.

4. John Calvin, *Commentaries on the Epistles to Timothy, Titus, and Philemon*, trans. William Pringle (Grand Rapids: Wm. B. Eerdmans Publishing Company, 1948), p. 77.

5. Will Durant, *The Story of Civilization: Caesar and Christ* (New York: Simon and Schuster, 1944), p. 396.

6. Charles Caldwell Ryrie, *You Mean the Bible Teaches That* (Chicago: Moody Press, 1974), p. 55.

9

Answers to Common Objections

As I have presented my views on divorce and remarriage to the seminary students I teach, I have found that not all agree with my position. I often smile and say, "I'm not asking you to agree, but you should know the arguments for this position in order to pass the exam!" Similarly, I am not asking you to accept every "jot and tittle" of my interpretations of the critical passages. All I ask is that you give this biblical approach to divorce and remarriage your thoughtful and prayerful consideration. But, perhaps you have some objections to the doctrine I have presented in the preceding chapters. I have designed this chapter just for you.

In my reading and study I have become convinced of the correctness of the views presented in this book. Yet I did not gain this understanding "overnight." I once held a very lenient view on divorce and remarriage and raised objections to such a strict view as that which I now affirm. So, be encouraged! I have stood in your shoes! This view is not without problems. There are legitimate objections which deserve to be answered. Having presented the biblical doctrine of divorce and remarriage as clearly as I am able, I would now like to answer what I believe to be the major objections of those who take a more lenient position on divorce and remarriage.

God's "Divorce" of Israel

In arguing for the position that divorce and remarriage

does not disqualify one from the office of pastor or deacon, it has been pointed out that God himself had a "divorce" (Hos. 2:2).[1] If *God* has been divorced, then certainly a Christian who has experienced a similar marital disaster should not be disqualified from church office. How does God's "divorce" apply to this contemporary issue of divorce and remarriage?

The prophet Hosea ministered at a spiritual low point during Israel's history. His prophecy is a testimony against the Northern Kingdom concerning its spiritual adultery and moral corruption. His very marriage to the unfaithful Gomer is a living illustration of Israel's unfaithfulness and God's unceasing love for His people. In Hosea 2:2 the individual members of the nation are commanded to contend with their "mother"—that is, the apostate nation of Israel. The Lord then declares, "She is not my wife, and I am not her husband." The point God is making is that as adultery destroys marriage, so idolatry destroys the intimate and unique relationship between God and His people. Yet in the same chapter God promises that the relationship between Him and His people will be renewed. This renewal is pictured as a marriage (Hos. 2:19, 20). Three times it is said that God will betroth Israel to himself. This of course will take place when Israel is redeemed as a nation (Rom. 11:26).

Later, through the prophet Jeremiah, the Lord declares concerning the Northern Kingdom of Israel, "And I saw that for all the adulteries of faithless Israel, I had sent her away and given her a writ of divorce" (Jer. 3:8). Because of the Northern Kingdom's violations of the conditional Mosaic Covenant, God sent His people away into exile (722 B.C.). They were separated or "divorced" from the land, the Temple, and the worship institutions of Israel. This "divorce," however, was certainly figurative rather than literal, for several verses later God declares, "Turn, O backsliding children . . . for I am married unto you" (Jer. 3:14, KJV). Through the prophet Isaiah the Lord points out that Israel's separation from God was a result of the people's own sin and not because God had forsaken them. The Lord asks, "Where is the certificate of divorce, by which I have sent your mother away?" (Isa. 50:1). To this question a negative answer is expected.[2] God has not dissolved His relationship with Israel. He is simply using divorce imagery to describe how this relationship has been corrupted by Israel's apostasy—her spiritual adultery.

We find in the Old Testament the apostate nation of Israel personified as an adulterous woman (Jer. 3:1, 3-10; 4:30; Ezek. 16, 23). As an adulterous wife is unfaithful to her husband, so Israel had been unfaithful to the Lord. Hosea says this apostasy has severed the relationship between God and Israel (Hos. 2:2). In Jeremiah God declares that He has given Israel a bill of divorcement, while in another context He calls into question the existence of a divorce document (Jer. 3:8; Isa. 50:1).

Obviously the concept of divorce is being used in a metaphorical sense when used to describe the relationship of God to Israel. The metaphor is designed to illustrate the condition of Israel's relationship with God resulting from the nation's apostasy. In fact, because of the Abrahamic Covenant (Gen. 12:2-3; 15:7-21; 17:7) the relationship between God and Israel can never be severed. God has unconditionally and unilaterally bound himself to the people of Israel.

The metaphor of divorce used to describe the condition of God's relationship with Israel was not designed to signify God's approval of divorce as a viable option for those experiencing marital difficulties. It would be a very incorrect application of the metaphor, for it contradicts the clear teaching of the more doctrinal passages in Scripture which speak directly to the issue. Since God's "divorce of Israel" is metaphorical, there is no implication that a divorced be-

liever would be biblically qualified for the office of pastor/
elder or deacon.

The Implication of "Apoluō"

It has been argued by some that the words used for divorce in the Old and New Testaments signify the thought of
dissolution with the right to remarriage for both partners
implied.[3] Granted, the Hebrew word for divorce (*kerithuth*)
is literally "a cutting off" and a bill of divorcement was a
"bill of cutting off." The Greek word for divorce (*apoluō*)
means "to set free" or "to release."[4] However, while the
biblical words for "divorce" may mean "to cut off" or "to
set free," mere legal divorce does not dissolve the marriage
union in an absolute sense before God. Let me explain.

The context is always the key to the meaning of a word.
Jesus' basic teaching is that *legal* divorce and *legal* remarriage is *biblical* adultery—except in the case of *porneia*. In
other words, while divorce may be legally executed, a marriage in God's eyes is a lifelong union and continues to exist
even when divorce has occurred. This is evidenced by Jesus'
words in Luke 16:18, "Every one who divorces his wife and
marries another commits adultery; and he who marries one
who is divorced from a husband commits adultery." Note
that this is a universal statement. Jesus says, "every one."
Divorce clearly does not dissolve the marriage, otherwise
Jesus would not have taught that remarriage results in
adultery.

Hence, when a divorced person remarries, adultery
takes place, for the original marriage union is violated by
the intrusion of a third person. Only in the case of *porneia*—a marriage within the forbidden degrees of kinship—could the marriage be dissolved in an absolute sense,
leaving both partners free to remarry. Scripture clearly
teaches that marriage is a lifelong relationship—binding
until death (Rom. 7:2-3; 1 Cor. 7:39).

The "Husbands" of the Samaritan Woman

In arguing that legal divorce implies the dissolution of
the marriage with the right of both partners to remarry, it
has been pointed out that Jesus recognized the legality of
the five marriages of the Samaritan woman (John 4:18).
Duty remarks, "Jesus seems to have given recognition to
the legality of the fact that the woman had been married to
'five husbands' (v. 18). This was a clear distinction of marital status."[5] Does the use of the term "husbands" by Jesus
actually imply His recognition and approval of the five
marriages?

In His conversation with the Samaritan woman at the
well, Jesus points the woman to her sin and her need for repentance. By His words in John 4:17-18 Jesus reveals that
He knows all about the woman's misadventures. He knows
that she had had *five* husbands and that the man with
whom she was now living was not legally her husband!
There is no reason to doubt that these five marriages were
legal according to rabbinic law. The lax divorce laws of the
time of Christ probably account for the woman's five marriages. While a woman could not divorce her husband according to Jewish law, under certain circumstances she
could go to court to compel her husband to divorce her or
even pay him to grant her a divorce.[6] In theory, there was
no limit to the number of marriages that might be contract-
ed after valid divorces according to rabbinic law, but the
rabbis regarded two or at the most three marriages as the
maximum for a woman.[7]

The lax divorce and remarriage laws of the Jews in the
first century are set in stark contrast with the teaching of
Jesus who affirmed that the marriage union must not be
broken (Matt. 19:6; Mark 10:9) and that divorce and remarriage constitute adultery—except in the case of *porneia*. Obviously, Jesus' teachings are quite different from

the Samaritan woman's practices. In John 4:18 Jesus is no doubt saying to the woman, "You have been married to five different men, when God's original plan was one partner for life, and you are now sexually involved with a sixth!" The statement was made to direct the woman to her sin and her need for Christ's provision of salvation. He was not in any way approving those five marriages. On the contrary, He was condemning them. They may have been legal according to Jewish rabbinic law, but they were not right according to God's revelation! Jesus was not recognizing marriage as "dissolved" by divorce in his reference to the Samaritan woman's five husbands. He was bringing the woman's sin into the open so that she might be convicted over what she knew in her own heart to be wrong.

The "Divine Provision" for Remarriage

In considering the teaching of Moses on divorce and remarriage in Deuteronomy 24:1-4, it has been argued that if divorce does not dissolve marriage, then God allowed adulterous remarriage and the illegitimacy of children born in the remarriage.[8] The key to answering this objection is to recognize that Deuteronomy 24 does not institute divorce, but merely treats it as a practice already known and existing. This legislation given through Moses was designed to protect the rejected wife and to give her certain safeguards and freedom from interference by the former husband in the case of a subsequent marriage. The passage speaks to a particular case of remarriage after a second marriage. Moses is saying that a man may not remarry his former wife if she has in the meantime married another man (Deut. 24:3-4). Even though her second husband should divorce her or die, she must not under any circumstances return to her first husband. To do so would be an abomination before the Lord and would bring the defilement of sin upon the land.

Quite obviously divorce and remarriage was taking

place in the time of Moses, hence this legislation was given in response to a particular need. However, according to the Old Testament, divorce and remarriage did not meet with God's *approval*. The prophet Malachi records the Lord's words, "For I hate divorce" (2:16). God is certainly not condoning in Deuteronomy what He clearly condemns in Malachi. We distinguish at this point between God's permissive will and God's preceptive will—between what God permits and what God prescribes. Divorce and remarriage in the Old Testament period was permitted by God, but not prescribed; allowed, but not commanded. Divorce and remarriage is contrary to God's original plan for marriage (Gen. 2:24) and Christ's teaching that the marriage union should not be severed (Matt. 19:6; Mark 10:9). Divorce, Jesus explains, is due to man's sinful and hard-hearted rejection of God's plan that marriage be permanent until death (Matt. 19:8; cf. 1 Cor. 7:39).

The progress of revelation also helps us understand why God did not declare in Deuteronomy 24 that divorce and remarriage resulted in adultery. God has progressively revealed himself and His program through the ages. It was over a period of 1,500 years that God revealed the great doctrines of salvation, the nature of man and last things. So, too, we see a progressive revelation of God's attitude toward divorce. In Genesis 2:24 God revealed His plan for marriage—one wife for life. After the Fall men turned from God's plan and instituted divorce and remarriage. In Deuteronomy 24:1-4 God sought to limit the rampant divorce of the Mosaic period, and disallowed remarriage in certain circumstances. In Malachi 2:16 God revealed His hatred for divorce. Through Jesus God revealed that divorce and remarriage in most circumstances constitutes adultery (Matt. 19:1-12; Mark 10:1-12; Luke 16:18). Finally, Paul confirms the teaching of Jesus and adds some further instruction to the divorced—remain single or be reconciled (1 Cor. 7:10-16). God did not reveal all the truth at once, but *progressively* revealed His desire for His people as further instruction was necessary. God's standard—no divorce—is unchanging. But the scriptural revelation of His dealing with this matter is progressive. Moses starts with the basics; Jesus directs us to the key issue; and Paul gives us the details.

Divorce and remarriage in the Old Testament is never called "adultery" (though God does label it "treachery" in Malachi 2:10-16). Divorce and remarriage is, nevertheless, contrary to God's plan for marriage. It certainly constitutes sin, for it is something that God hates. Divorce and remarriage was recognized by the *people* of Israel, but it did not have the approval of the *God* of Israel. According to rabbinic law, divorce did dissolve the marriage and permission for remarriage was implied. But according to Christ's teaching, mere legal divorce does not dissolve marriage, and remarriage constitutes adultery. The progressive revelation of this doctrine helps us understand the difference between what is recorded in the Old Testament and what is required in the New Testament. God's attitude toward divorce has never changed, but His revelation of His dealings with divorce and divorced persons is progressive.

The Need for Fulfillment in Life

I recently had the opportunity to share my approach to divorce and remarriage with a friend of mine who is a pastor. His primary objection to my view was that it could not be applied to the lives of his people. The point he made was that God wants Christians to be fulfilled, and divorced people who desire marriage will not be fulfilled and satisfied apart from having a husband or wife, and a family.

In response to this objection let me say again that a strict interpretation of the divorce text will not be easy to apply because it means that some people who want to be divorced will have to stay married, and others who want to remarry will have to stay single. Some people might think that they cannot be "fulfilled" living as a single person without the companionship and sexual outlet that marriage provides. However, *where in the Bible is married life equated with Christian fulfillment*? Did Paul not prefer the single life because it provided opportunity for undistracted devotion to the Lord (1 Cor. 7:7, 32-35)? Is the sexual experience which marriage provides necessary for a fulfilled life? It is important to remember that while Christ promised an "abundant" life to those who trusted Him (John 10:10), He never promised happiness and every other thing we might want. On the contrary, Christ promised hardship, persecution, and hostility from the world (John 15:18-25; 16:1-4). Being a Christian and following Christ's teaching is not easy. It takes courage and commitment. Yet like Paul, a committed Christian finds Christ's grace sufficient to see him through the trials and testings of life (2 Cor. 12:9).

Margaret Clarkson is an author and poet from Willowdale, Ontario. She has been single all her life and testifies that while it has not been easy, it has been possible.

> Through no fault or choice of my own, I am unable to express sexuality in the beauty and intimacy of Christian marriage, as God intended when he created me a sexual being in his own image. To seek to do this outside of marriage is, by the clear teaching of Scripture, to sin against God and against my own nature. As a committed Christian, then, I have no alternative but to live a life of voluntary celibacy. I must be chaste not only in body, but in mind and spirit as well. Since I am now in my 60's, I think that my experience of what this means is valid. I want to go on record as having proved that for those who are committed to do God's will, his commands are his enablings.[9]

God's commands are His enablings! If you are single due to divorce, know that God will sustain you and minister to you as a single. Don't compromise the teachings of the Bible to justify remarriage just so you can be "fulfilled." Know that the single life can be a fulfilling experience for you as you obey God and trust Him to enable you to live for Him.

Summary and Conclusion

In John 8:31-32 Jesus said to those who had believed on Him, "If you abide in My word, then you are truly disciples of Mine; and you shall know the truth, and the truth shall make you free." These words have encouraged me greatly as I have sought God's truth in many important areas of doctrine. Following Christ's teaching will prove we are genuine disciples and will open the door to God's truth which brings true spiritual freedom. Christ's disciples have no reason to fear the truth. For this reason I have not hesitated to question my own convictions in certain doctrinal matters, asking, "Do my beliefs match up with the teachings of the Word of God?" Raising objections to particular views is healthy and profitable, for if the objections can be adequately answered, the view is strengthened. If they cannot be adequately answered, then further study is necessary in our search for the truth. Fortunately we are not in this search alone, for God has provided the Holy Spirit and gifted teachers to help us understand the truth of His Word (John 16:13; Eph 4:11).

In this chapter I have sought to answer the major objections that have been raised against what I believe to be the biblical teaching on divorce and remarriage. Perhaps not all the objections that *could* be raised have been dealt with, but if these major objections can be adequately answered, certainly lesser objections pose no major threat to this position.

The clear teaching of the Word of God is that marriage was divinely designed to be a lifelong union of a couple as husband and wife. While divorce did take place both in the Old Testament and the New Testament eras, it never met with God's approval. Divorce and remarriage is something God hates! To say that God condones what He clearly condemns in His Word is to make God contradict himself—something impossible for an unchanging God to do. While there are some objections to the "no divorce" position set forth in this book, they are not without reasonable answers. Some who raise such objections are merely "grasping at straws" in an attempt to justify their own or others' actions. Such objections do not in any significant way undermine the clear and authoritative teaching of the Word of God that marriage is for life!

Study Questions

1. Have you ever initially rejected a doctrine or teaching which you later discovered to be true? Give one example.
2. What assurance does the believer have that God's truth is "knowable" (John 16:13; 17:17)? What agents does God use to bring us to a knowledge of His truth?
3. Why is it a healthy and profitable exercise to review, re-evaluate, and even raise objections to certain doctrines we have been taught?
4. Does God's "divorce" of Israel mean that a divorced individual should not be disqualified from the office of elder or deacon? Is the metaphor of divorce designed to signify God's approval of divorce as a viable option for those experiencing marital difficulties?
5. Does the Greek word for divorce signify the complete dissolution of the marriage with the right to remarriage for both partners implied? Why or why not?
6. Does the use of the term "husbands" by Jesus in John 4:18 imply His recognition and approval of the Samaritan woman's five marriages? Explain your answer.
7. How does the "progress of revelation" help us understand why God did not declare in Deuteronomy 24 that divorce and remarriage results in adultery?
8. Is the "need for fulfillment" in life a reasonable objection to the biblical view on divorce and remarriage

presented in this book? Is marriage essential to a fulfilled and abundant life? How would the Apostle Paul have answered this question?

Notes

1. Stanley A. Ellisen, *Divorce and Remarriage in the Church* (Grand Rapids: Zondervan Publishing Company, 1977), pp. 18, 84.

2. Edward J. Young, *The Book of Isaiah*, 3 vols., The New International Commentary (Grand Rapids: Wm. B. Eerdmans Publishing Co., 1972), vol. 1, p. 295.

3. Guy Duty, *Divorce and Remarriage* (Minneapolis, Minnesota: Bethany Fellowship, Inc., 1967), p. 39.

4. *A Manual Greek Lexicon of the New Testament*, ed. G. Abbott-Smith, s.v. "Apoluō," p. 53.

5. Duty, *Divorce and Remarriage*, p. 28.

6. *Ketuvot* 7:9, *Gittin* 7:5, 6.

7. Leon Morris, *The Gospel According to John*, The New International Commentary on the New Testament (Grand Rapids: Wm. B. Eerdmans Publishing Company, 1971), p. 264, n. 43.

8. Duty, *Divorce and Remarriage*, p. 130.

9. Margaret Clarkson, "Singleness: His Share for Me," *Christianity Today* (February 16, 1979), pp. 14-15.

10

How to Apply the Doctrine Practically

The biblical teaching on divorce and remarriage is not just theoretical, but is applicable in the lives of believers. But at this point you might be saying, "A strict view on divorce and remarriage is going to be hard to apply to the lives of people who are physical and emotional beings." Right you are! It is much easier for me to teach this doctrine in a seminary classroom than to present it to a divorced person who is contemplating remarriage. My desire to be appreciated and to make people happy has sometimes conflicted with my convictions regarding divorce and remarriage. I recall when I recently delivered a message in a local church on Jesus' teaching on divorce and remarriage. Afterward, a young woman who had been attending services regularly came and told me that seven years ago she had been divorced. Now she was growing in the Lord and wanted to get married. She wanted to know what she should do. I wanted so much to be able to tell her to go ahead and get married—but I could not do so in light of my biblical convictions. Had my convictions not been firmly grounded in the Scriptures, I am sure I would have yielded to my feelings and the pressure of the situation.

Another thought that has probably crossed your mind is, "Surely only a hard-nosed old celibate Bible scholar without feelings for the needs of people could ever hold to such an interpretation of the divorce and remarriage texts!" I have seen friends, fellow church members, and relatives suffer the tragedy of a marital failure. I have endured sleepless nights contemplating the situations of the people involved. My convictions have not come to me from a vacuum of experience or in an isolated ivory tower. I have great sympathy for the plight of divorced people, but I must be loyal to what the Bible teaches on this vital subject. I trust that my application of this doctrine to the lives of God's people will reflect not only His holiness, but also His love, grace, mercy, and compassion. I believe that the following question-and-answer approach will be the best way to make application of this biblical doctrine.

1. *What is marriage from a biblical standpoint? What constitutes divorce? How does culture and the law of the land bear on this question?* Marriage is basically the legal union of a man and woman as husband and wife. According to Genesis 2:24, three basic elements are involved: (1) a public act expressing the intent of the couple, (2) a permanent bonding of two lives together, and (3) a physical union consummating the relationship. The term is also used of the ceremony initiating and celebrating that union. While marriage was God-ordained and blessed (Gen. 2:23-24; John 2:1-11), it is essentially a state-recognized domestic institution. Divorce, on the other hand, is the legal dissolution of the marriage. Since divorce was not instituted by God, it is in almost every circumstance not recognized by Him; hence, divorce and remarriage is adultery since the original marriage is still intact from God's perspective.

The culture and laws of the land really determine what is recognized as marriage and what constitutes divorce. Customs differ from country to country. The essential issue is, "What is recognized as legal marriage in this land?" In Germany the legal marriage is performed by a state magistrate, and the church ceremony is just a formality. The church wedding alone would not constitute a legal marriage in that country. Since God has given man the authority to govern (Rom. 13:1-7), the laws concerning legal marriage and legal divorce are to be determined by the state.

2. *What does it mean to become "one flesh"? Is becoming "one flesh" the same as becoming married?* Leupold has suggested that becoming one flesh "involves the complete identification of one personality with the other in a community of interests and pursuits, a union consummated in intercourse."[1] This definition can hardly be improved upon. Becoming "one flesh" physically does not make a marriage, for marriage is an institution recognized by the state, and certain elements must be present and proper procedures must be followed for a relationship to qualify. Notice that Jesus does not refer to the man with whom the Samaritan woman was living as her "husband" (John 4:18). She had been legally married to five different husbands, but was now involved in an illicit affair. Mere sexual intercourse does not make a marriage. On the other hand, there is no sexual intercourse that does not result in the two becoming one flesh (cf. 1 Cor. 6:16).

The "one flesh" that a married couple becomes is beautifully illustrated in the children God gives them. In a child, father and mother are indissolubly united into one person. Though divorce should take place, the "one flesh" relationship still exists, and continues to be illustrated in one's offspring. Anything that violates or intrudes upon that unique "one flesh" relationship shared by a married couple, whether Christian or not, is adulterous and a violation of God's marriage law.

3. *Are there any legitimate, biblical grounds for divorce—adultery, desertion, wife beating, mental cruelty, or incest?* Since God hates divorce (Mal. 2:16), and Jesus commanded that it be stopped (Matt. 19:6; Mark 10:9), and Paul four times declared that there should be no divorce (1 Cor. 7:10-13), I would have to say that there are no legitimate, biblical grounds for divorce. God's original de-

sign for marriage is one partner for life! Jesus taught that divorce and remarriage results in adultery in every circumstance except in the case of *porneia*, which we determined to refer to marriage within the prohibited relationships of Leviticus 18:6-18. As tragic as marital infidelity, desertion, and wife beating may be, they do not constitute biblical grounds for divorce. These were all first-century problems that Jesus could have addressed and made allowances for, but He did not choose to do so. We would do well to follow His example!

4. *Do the terms "innocent party" and "guilty party" have significance in the biblical teaching on divorce and remarriage?* These terms are used by those who see divorce and remarriage as permissible in the case of adultery and perhaps desertion. The "innocent party" is the spouse who has been wronged, and the "guilty party" is the spouse who has been unfaithful or has abandoned the other partner. According to my strict approach on the subject of divorce and remarriage, these terms have little application.

In a sense there is no "innocent" or "guilty" party in a marital break-up. It takes two to make a marriage and it usually takes two to make a divorce. While one partner may be the major contributor to the difficulties, it is hard for me to designate the other partner "innocent." Did that spouse seek counsel early when the problems first began to appear? Did that spouse love unconditionally and sacrificially in such a way as to make the home and family life as pleasant as possible? If infidelity has taken place, did the "innocent" party forgive and forget? Divorce results from the failure of two people to honor their mutual covenant to stay by one another's side until death. In a real sense, then, there is no "innocent" party in a divorce—only a husband and wife who are both guilty of failing to fulfill their covenant promise to each other.

5. *If a divorce should occur before one is saved, does this change matters?* Some have argued that since everyone be-

comes a new creature in Christ (2 Cor. 5:17), one who has been divorced prior to becoming a Christian should be entitled to another marriage as a believer. However, it is important to recognize that while the guilt of sin is entirely forgiven at the time of salvation (Rom. 8:1), the consequences of that sin in this present life are not necessarily removed. A thief who is saved in prison is not automatically released. A legal contract to purchase a house is not altered by one of the parties becoming a Christian. David was forgiven his sin with Bathsheba immediately upon confession (2 Sam. 12:13; Ps. 51), but nevertheless bore the consequences of the sin in his life (2 Sam. 12:14-15). Likewise, while divorce (and remarriage) are forgivable sins, they may have lifelong consequences. According to Paul's teaching, a marriage union is not altered in any way by one of the partners becoming a Christian (1 Cor. 7:12-13). Similarly, God's will for one who is divorced before being saved is reconciliation with the original partner, not a new marriage (1 Cor. 7:11). Interestingly, Jesus gave His teaching on divorce and remarriage to unbelieving Pharisees (Matt. 19:3; Mark 10:2). Apparently one lifelong marriage is God's standard for *society*, not just for the church!

6. *Is separation without the dissolution of the marriage a possible solution for those experiencing marital difficulties?* While the continuation of the marriage is always God's will (Matt. 19:6; Mark 10:9), I believe that a temporary separation may be helpful in avoiding further difficulties while the couple is receiving marital counseling. Such a separation may be necessary in order to ensure the safety and well-being of a wife who is married to a violent, alcoholic husband. Any such separation should always be with a view to reconciliation and the continuation of the marriage relationship.

7. *Should divorced persons or those separated due to marital difficulties date anyone other than the alienated spouse?* Since God's will is always reconciliation to one's

spouse, dating is completely out of place for divorced or separated persons. Dating can only lead to emotional involvements which will make reconciliation more difficult. Such dating sometimes results in a triangle love affair and even adultery which further undermines a marriage and limits the chances for reconciliation. The only way to encourage marital reconciliation is for divorced and separated persons not to date anyone other than their original spouse.

8. *Should a man or woman divorce a second spouse in order to go back to the original partner?* Divorce and remarriage must be recognized as sin—but sin that can be forgiven. When a divorced person comes to the realization as a Christian that a sin has taken place in his or her life, it should be confessed as sin and God's cleansing can then be appropriated (1 John 1:9). If a second marriage has taken place, it should not be dissolved in order to return to one's previous spouse. Deuteronomy 24:1-4 speaks to this issue. To return to one's first spouse after divorce and remarriage to a second is declared by Moses to be "an abomination before the Lord" (Deut. 24:4). Why? Because if this were permitted, divorce and remarriage would become a "legal" form of committing adultery. If you have been divorced and remarried, recognize it as sin and appropriate God's cleansing and forgiveness, but do not compound the sin by destroying a second marriage in order to re-establish the first.

9. *Is a person who has been divorced and remarried living in a state of continual adultery?* Jesus declares in Mark 10:11-12 that "whoever divorces his wife and marries another woman commits adultery against her; and if she herself divorces her husband and marries another man, she is committing adultery." The present tense of the verb "commits adultery" (*moichatai*) is used in both occurrences. While the present is the normal tense used to represent durative or continuous action, there is an aoristic use of the present which presents punctiliar action in the present time. The aoristic present is used for expressing the idea of a present

fact or an event as now occurring.[2] Hence, the present tense "commits adultery" could refer to a continued state of adultery or simply a one-time act of adultery. The context of the passage, which contains a succession of aorists, and the prohibition against returning to one's former spouse after a second marriage, would point in the direction of the second view. Jesus was probably teaching His disciples that the act of divorcing one's spouse and marrying another was at that moment an act of adultery. Divorced and remarried persons would not be considered to be living in a state of continual adultery.

10. *Does a person who has not been previously married commit adultery should he or she marry a divorcée?* In Luke 16:18 Jesus says, "Everyone who divorces his wife and marries another commits adultery; and he who marries one who is divorced from a husband commits adultery." Since the God-ordained marriage union is lifelong, to marry a divorced person would be to enter into an existing marriage and hence, to commit adultery.

11. *Why is divorce considered greater than other sins in disqualifying a person from the office of elder or deacon?* Divorce is not really a greater sin than any other, but it is a more *public* sin. Recall Nathan's words to David after his sin of adultery with Bathsheba, "Because by this deed you have given occasion to the enemies of the Lord to blaspheme, the child also that is born to you shall surely die" (2 Sam. 12:14). Public sin has public consequences! As disobedience disqualified Saul from kingship (1 Sam. 15:22-23), so also the violation of God's marriage standard disqualifies one from office in the local church.

12. *Would a believer who was divorced but later reconciled and remarried to his original spouse meet the marriage qualifications for the office of pastor/elder or deacon?* The marriage qualification for elder and deacon is that the man, if married, must be the "husband of one wife." The phrase refers to one who has been married to just *one* wife

and has been totally devoted to her. A believer who was divorced, but later reconciled to his spouse could *possibly* qualify for church office. Several factors should be considered. First, was there any immorality associated with the divorce? If so, the husband would not be "above reproach" (1 Tim. 3: 2, 10). Second, is he presently managing his household well and keeping his children well behaved? If not, how would he be qualified to take care of God's church (1 Tim. 3:4, 5)? Third, has sufficient time passed since the divorce and remarriage for the husband to prove himself worthy of church office (1 Tim. 3:10)? I would suggest that a divorced believer who has been reconciled and remarried to his wife be carefully examined before being appointed to church office. Only if he is deemed "above reproach"— blameless in all areas of his family life—would he qualify for the office of elder or deacon.

13. *Why is the marriage union so sacred to God and indissoluble?* I do not claim to have the final or complete answer to this question, but let me suggest this thought. In Ephesians 5:22-33 Paul expounds on the marriage relationship between husband and wife. The wife is to submit to her husband as the church submits to Christ, and the husband is to love his wife as Christ sacrificially loved the church. While Paul is referring to the marriage relationship, his discussion really centers on the relationship between Christ and the church (Eph. 5:32). Paul points out in Ephesians 5:32 that there marriage has a symbolic purpose. The marriage union is designed to reflect the relationship between Christ and His church. Just as a union is formed in marriage when two people commit their lives to each other, so a union is formed when the believer is joined to Christ as he trusts Him for salvation. Will Christ ever break the relationship between himself and His church? Absolutely not (Heb. 13:5)! Will Christ ever be "divorced" or separated from the believer? Never (Rom. 8:35-39; John 10:28)! Since the marriage union is a picture of the permanent relation-

ship between Christ and His church, the marriage union itself must be permanent. If marriage were a dissoluble relationship, it would be an inaccurate representation of the indissoluble relationship between Christ and His church.

14. *What deterrents are there to divorce?* One of the strongest deterrents to divorce is *positive instruction* concerning God's plan for the permanence of marriage. As long as Christians view divorce as a possible way out of their marital problems, many struggling couples will follow that route. Instead of seeking to resolve their differences biblically, they will file for divorce. Such a course of action reflects a wrong view of marriage—the "marriage is bliss" syndrome. Many misinformed married couples think that the primary purpose of marriage is to make them happy. It's not! Marriage is designed by God to provide for the procreation and raising of children (Gen. 1:28; Eph. 6:1-4); to provide companionship and intimate fellowship for man (Gen. 2:18); and to reflect the relationship between Christ and His church (Eph. 5:31-32). In addition, marriage is a kind of "sandpaper" that God uses to smooth the rough edges off believers and thus bring them into conformity with the image of His Son (cf. Rom. 8:29). Being "sanded" by God does not always make us happy. However, happiness and bliss in marriage is like the cherry on the chocolate sundae—it is very nice, but not absolutely necessary. Enjoy the cherry if it's there, but don't throw away the sundae just because it's not!

Another significant deterrent to divorce would be the interpretation of the divorce and remarriage texts I have shared with you in this book. I am convinced that if a strict view on divorce and remarriage were taught in our churches, there would be fewer divorces among believers. Marriage would be entered into with more caution, and marriage partners would seek to preserve that union at all cost, for there would be no second chance. If for no other reason, a husband's sexual needs will motivate him to maintain the marriage in a healthy condition, for if he fails he will be left to a single life! Counseling Christian young people and engaged couples concerning the permanence and inviolability of the marriage union would certainly deter divorce. I personally refuse to perform a wedding for a couple who believes that divorce is a viable option for believers experiencing marital difficulties.

15. *How should a local church respond toward a couple who have rejected the pastor's counsel regarding remarriage, have gone to another pastor to be married, and then returned to the church for fellowship?* James points out in his epistle that "to one who knows the right thing to do, and does not do it, to him it is sin" (James 4:17). According to the position set forth in this book, divorce and remarriage constitutes a sin against God and is a manifestation of disobedience to his Word. It is significant, I believe, that the Old Testament distinguishes between an inadvertent or unintentional sin and the defiant sin (where one who knows God's law wills to violate it). The Hebrew text of Numbers 15:30 refers to this latter kind of sin as "the sin of the high hand." God made provision for atoning sacrifice in the case of the unintentional sin (Num. 15:22-29), but there was no sacrifice possible in the case of the "sin of the high hand." The one who knowingly and intentionally violated God's law would be "cut off from among his people"—that is, put to death (Num. 15:30; cf. Ex 31:14). My point here is that I would consider it rather dangerous to knowingly disobey God's Word. I am not saying that such a sin cannot be forgiven, but that to so presume upon God's grace would be to provoke His wrath! If those involved are true believers, we can be assured that they will be the recipients of God's disciplinary judgment (cf. Heb. 12:6-11; 13:4).

In dealing with such a couple, I believe that the instructions of Jesus in Matthew 18:15-17 should be followed. The first step would be that of private reproof by the pastor or an appointed elder. In a compassionate and loving way, the sin should be pointed out and repentance requested. If there is no repentance, the second step should be to have the couple meet with the pastors, elders, or deacons (depending on your church polity) for the purpose of pointing out the sin and calling for repentance. If the couple still refuses to acknowledge their wrong, then the matter should go before the whole church at a special meeting of the body. If there is still no response on the couple's part, then, following the instructions of Jesus, the couple should be separated from fellowship with the local body of believers. This can be done by removing their names from the church role and (or) denying them the privilege of sharing in the Lord's Supper. Should there be a manifestation of genuine repentance at any step in the disciplinary process, the couple should be restored to *full* fellowship with the members of the church. It should be acknowledged, however, that divorce and remarriage would limit the couple in certain areas of Christian service.

Denying fellowship to a sinning Christian is a weighty step for any local church to take, yet the Apostle Paul in dealing with the church at Corinth indicates that this is sometimes necessary (cf. 1 Cor. 5:1-13). Note, however, that separation from fellowship should not be viewed as an end in itself. Such discipline is designed to lead the sinner to repentance! Paul emphasizes that when the discipline has served its purpose, the repentant sinner ought to be forgiven, comforted, and brought back into fellowship with the local body (cf. 2 Cor. 2:5-8). Paul points out to the Corinthians the *danger* of an unforgiving spirit—it invites Satan to take advantage of the situation and promote his evil designs (2 Cor. 2:10-11).

The greatest temptation for believers in dealing with those who have knowingly violated God's design for marriage is to withhold forgiveness. You might say to yourself, "Why, they recognized that remarriage was wrong but did it anyway because they knew the church could forgive them." Well, that may be true. But only the omniscient God can make such a judgment. We as Christians cannot deny such a couple the forgiveness that God grants (cf. Matt. 6:14-15; 18:21-35). When you are confronted with this situation, avoid being judgmental. Pray that Christ will manifest His compassion in your own heart. Stand by to counsel the couple concerning their need for repentance. Be ready to minister as God takes the couple through His program of divine discipline which will ultimately produce in them the "peaceful fruit of righteousness" (Heb. 12:11).

16. *What should be the Christian's attitude toward divorcées and toward divorced and remarried persons?* In dealing with divorcées and divorced and remarried persons, Christians ought to reflect God's attitude of love, compassion, sympathy, forgiveness, and acceptance. While God said, "I hate divorce," He never said, "I hate divorcées!" He hates the sin, but loves the sinner.

I do not believe that we as Christians should condone any sin—and divorce is no exception. But on the other hand, we must not condemn those who have suffered a marital failure. We must leave judgment in such matters to God (Rom. 14:10-12). Rather than shunning divorced persons, Christians should make a special effort to include them in church activities and make them feel accepted as a part of the fellowship.

One of my best friends is divorced and remarried. We went to seminary together and have ministered together. We have enjoyed fellowship on frequent fishing trips and woodcutting outings. We have openly discussed our views on divorce and remarriage with each other. Although we disagree with each other's conclusions, we appeal to the same source of authority—the Word of God. Our relationship is characterized not only by mutual respect, but by genuine brotherly love. I think the real keys to our good relationship are honesty and mutual acceptance. I believe that God will be glorified and the unity of the church will be strengthened as believers reflect Christ's attitude of love and acceptance toward divorcées and divorced and remarried persons.

Summary and Conclusion

I believe there are two keys to the practical application of the biblical approach to divorce and remarriage. First, we must make our decisions and give our counsel not on the basis of what we think or feel, but *according to what the Bible says*. God's Word clearly teaches that marriage is for life. Only upon the death of a spouse is one free to remarry. Divorce and remarriage while the first spouse yet lives constitutes adultery. For the divorced believer there are basically two options—reconciliation or the single life. Most decisions relative to divorce and remarriage can be made on the basis of this plain and simple truth revealed in the Word of God.

The second key, I believe, to the practical application of this doctrine is in *"speaking the truth in love"* (Eph. 4:15). It is not so much *what* we say, but *how* we say it that often offends people and makes truth hard to swallow. I am reminded of the story of two preachers who came to town and both preached on hell. The first preacher received a very poor response and nobody appreciated his ministry. The second preacher was well received and there was a good response to his ministry. What made the difference? The first preacher preached as if he wanted everybody to go to hell, while the second man preached as if he didn't want anyone to go there! I believe we can speak God's truth on divorce and remarriage "in love"—with a tenderness and compassion which will enable people to graciously receive and apply the truth.

Study Questions

1. According to the Bible, would adultery, desertion, wife beating, mental cruelty, or incest be grounds for divorce? Why not?

2. If a divorce should occur before one is saved, is that person entitled to another marriage as a believer? Explain your answer.

3. Are there any circumstances in which separation without the dissolution of the marriage would seem advisable?

4. Why would it be very unwise for divorced or separated persons to date anyone other than the alienated spouse?

5. Why would it not be right for a man or woman to divorce a second spouse in order to go back to the former partner?

6. Is a person who has been divorced and remarried living in a state of continual adultery? Why not?

7. Does a person who has not been previously married commit adultery if he or she marries a divorcée?

8. Why should divorce disqualify a man from the office of pastor/elder or deacon when other sins might not?

9. Why do you think the marriage union is so sacred to God and indissoluble?

10. What should be the Christian's attitude toward divorce? How should this differ from one's attitude toward divorcées?

Notes

1. H. C. Leupold, *Exposition of Genesis*, 2 vols. (Grand Rapids: Baker Book House, 1942), vol. i, p. 137.

2. H. E. Dana and J. R. Mantey, *A Manual Grammar of the Greek New Testament* (Toronto: The Macmillan Company, 1927), p. 184.

11

Divorce, Remarriage, and the Christian Counselor

It is virtually impossible for the Christian counselor to escape the question of divorce and remarriage. The number of divorces in America has increased 65% from 1970 to 1979.[1] Marital disaster has found its way into the homes of Christians and non-Christians alike. Many of those in the midst of divorce or contemplating remarriage will seek counsel from friends, a pastor, or perhaps a professional counselor. Unfortunately, much of this counsel, though offered out of sincere concern, contradicts the biblical teaching on divorce and remarriage.

A woman experiencing marital difficulties visited a Christian counselor I am acquainted with. The counselor mentioned that one possible solution to her problems was divorce. Well, this woman was not looking for a divorce—she just wanted help with her marriage. Consequently she never went back for further counsel! What kind of counsel should a Christian counselor give to someone in marital difficulty? How would you counsel a friend in the midst of a divorce or contemplating remarriage?

You may think that this chapter is primarily designed to benefit the professional counselor who had a degree in psychology, an office and clients who come for regular visits. No! This chapter is for *you*! Proverbs 27:9 says, "Oil and perfume make the heart glad, so a man's counsel is sweet to his friend." Throughout your life you will have the opportunity to counsel your friends, fellow workers and family members. Will your counsel be sweet as honey or sour as a lemon? People in need will come to you perhaps simply because you are a friend, or because they know that you are a Christian. They might approach you for help because they see that you have a happy marriage—the kind of marriage they would like for themselves. They will come to *you* for help! The principles set forth in this chapter can enable you to be an effective and successful Christian counselor to those contemplating divorce or remarriage.

Biblical Models for the Christian Counselor

You have often heard it said, "A picture is worth a thousand words." Although God did not coin this expression, He certainly acknowledges its truth. In communicating His Word to His people, God has presented us with some stories that paint pictures that are more expressive than a thousand words. These historical accounts in the Word of God give us, I believe, some biblical models to follow in dealing with those experiencing marital difficulties.

David and Nathan (2 Sam. 12). Second Samuel 12 records how Nathan, David's counselor, used a very pointed parable to bring David to condemn his own sin of adultery with Bathsheba and bring him to repentance. After David's sin with Bathsheba, Nathan was faced with the need to confront unrepentant David with his sin. He did this by telling David a parable about a rich man who robbed a poor man of his only lamb and killed it to feed a traveler (vv. 1-4). When David said that the rich man deserved to die for his sin (vv. 5-6), Nathan declared to David, "You are the man!" (v. 7). He then pointed out David's sin (v. 9) and pronounced God's judgment on David and his family (vv. 11-12). David's confession was immediate, as was God's gracious forgiveness (v. 13). The fuller expression of David's confession is found in Psalm 51.

Nathan's dealing with king David illustrates the principle that one responsibility of a counselor is to reprove sin. Paul exemplifies this in 1 Corinthians 5-6 where he reproves the Corinthian believers for their lack of church discipline, their lawsuits and their immorality. So, too, the Christian counselor has the responsibility to point out violations of scriptural commands. A simple and effective way to accomplish this is for the counselor to have the counselee read a portion of Scripture that relates to the issue. Then simply ask the question, "How does your present conduct or future plans relate to this teaching?" The Scripture will both reprove and correct the sinner (2 Tim. 3:16).

Some of us are afraid to confront our friends with their violations of God's commands. The wife of one of my students recently faced the dilemma of being asked to participate in the wedding of a girlfriend who was going to marry a divorced man. She knew she could not compromise her convictions and wondered how to handle this situation. Finally, she wrote to her friend and lovingly told her that her plans for marriage were not in keeping with God's Word, and that she would not take part in the ceremony. Such action took courage, but God will honor those who, like John the Baptist (cf. Matt. 14:4), are not afraid to call sin "sin."

Jesus and the adulterous woman (John 8). John 8:1-11 records Jesus' encounter with the adulterous woman. While some have raised questions about this portion of John's text, I believe that both internal and external evidence point to its authenticity.[2] Here we find a beautiful illustration of Christ's mercy, compassion and willingness to *forgive.* The woman taken in adultery was brought by the scribes and Pharisees to Jesus for His opinion as to her punishment. Notice that verse 6 reveals the religious leaders were "testing" Jesus. If He advocated death by stoning, He would be disregarding the policy of Rome (cf. John 18:31). But if He contradicted the Mosaic command for stoning (Lev. 20:10; Deut. 22: 22-24), they would consider Him disqualified from being Messiah. Either way, Jesus was going to face charges under Roman or Mosaic Law. So, he did not say anything; He just wrote in the dirt. He then turned the tables on the woman's accusers to show that they were equally guilty: "He who is without sin among you, let him be the first to throw a stone at her" (8:7). John records that one by one the accusers departed. Jesus then turned to the obviously repentant woman. "Did no one condemn you?" He asked. And she said, "No one, Lord." Then Jesus said, "Neither do I condemn you; go your way; from now on sin no more" (John 8:10-11).

Jesus' dealings with the adulterous woman illustrates the principle that God forgives *repentant* sinners. Jesus forgave the adulterous woman and He will forgive those who have broken their marriages and sinned by forming new unions while their former partners yet live. While the Christian counselor must call divorce and remarriage what it really is—sin—the counselor must also emphasize that Christ died for this sin and that cleansing and restoration to fellowship are available on the basis of 1 John 1:9, "If we confess our sins, He is faithful and righteous to forgive us our sins and to cleanse us from all unrighteousness."

Jesus and the Samaritan woman (John 4). John 4 records Jesus' encounter with the Samaritan woman at Jacob's well. The conversation recorded in John 4:7-26 illustrates how Jesus tactfully aroused the spiritual interest in an individual to bring that one to a sense of need for the Savior. There by Jacob's well in the heat of the day, Jesus asked the woman for a drink of water. He then began to raise the conversation from the physical to the spiritual plane. He told the Samaritan woman in verse 10 that if she knew the gift of God (i.e., salvation) and who He was (i.e., the Savior), then she would ask and receive "living water." Jesus later explained that this living water springs "up to eternal life" (v. 14). As a result of this conversation the woman apparently came to saving faith in Christ (v. 42).

Now, Jesus knew all along that this woman had a disastrous marital history. She had been married to five husbands and was now living with a man apart from the sanctions of marriage (v. 18). While Jesus could have started off by discussing her marital affairs, He preferred to first address her spiritual condition! Here we learn the principle that one's spiritual condition takes priority over one's marital situation. When counseling an unsaved friend experiencing marital problems, start with the basics—salvation in Christ. It will not do much good to try and patch up a marriage by dealing with the symptoms and neglecting the very *source* of the difficulty. God is concerned both for the spiritual condition of people and their marital problems as well, but spiritual needs take precedence. As a Christian counselor, first direct people to Christ, and then help them find a solution to their marital problems in Him!

The Lord and Hosea (Hosea 1-3). Of the marriages recorded in the Bible, there is probably none so tragic as that of Hosea, the prophet of God. The first word from the Lord to this prophet was a command for him to marry a woman who would later become a harlot (Hos. 1:2). Hosea's marriage was designed to be a picture of the relationship between God and His people Israel. The physical unfaithfulness of Hosea's wife, Gomer, would portray the spiritual unfaithfulness of Israel. Hosea married Gomer who probably remained faithful during the infancy of her three children and then fell into adultery and eventually into slavery (3:1-2).

Chapter 3 of Hosea is the most important chapter of the prophecy and contains one of the greatest expressions of God's unceasing love found anywhere in the Bible. Now remember, Hosea's marriage is designed to portray the Lord's relationship with His people. As Gomer had been unfaithful to Hosea, so had Israel been unfaithful to the Lord. In Hosea 3 we find Gomer, like Israel, in the deepest debauchery. She has been sold by her lovers into slavery! Now comes the word of the Lord to Hosea, "Go again, love a woman who is loved by her husband, yet an adulteress" (3:1). God was saying to Hosea, "Take her back; love her again; be reconciled in your relationship!" Hosea bought Gomer from the slave market for a mere fifteen shekels of silver and a basket of barley!

How would you have responded if you had been Hosea? "But, Lord, adultery is grounds for stoning, and you want me to take her back as a wife?" or, "Lord, how about a divorce? I'll marry some other woman for you!" or, "Then if you insist—no divorce, but how about at least a separation?" or, "What will all the people of Israel think of me?" Hosea raised no such objections. He simply recognized that God's will for his marriage was *reconciliation.* He again loved Gomer and illustrated to the people of his day God's unceasing love for His own unfaithful people of Israel.

The key principle we may glean from the Lord's dealings with Hosea is that *God's will for divorced or separated couples is always reconciliation.* Under no circumstances—no matter how gross—would it be God's will for divorce to take place. This principle is beautifully illustrated by Hosea and stated quite explicitly by Jesus (Matt. 19:6; Mark 10:9) and Paul (1 Cor. 7:10-16). The biblical models for the Christian counselor well illustrate the counselor's responsibility to point out sin, share God's forgiveness, lead people to Christ, and encourage reconciliation for separated couples.

Counseling Persons Considering Divorce

A friend of mine from another city called me a short time ago. After a good chat about matters of our common interest, I asked about his wife and family. "That's one of the reasons I called, " he said. "I don't know how much longer Betty is going to be with me. She has become involved with another man and I'm considering divorce." After recovering from the initial shock of this news, I began to think of how I might help my friend and counsel him in light of his difficult marital situation. In this section I will present the guidelines I have developed for counseling persons considering divorce. Remember, these are guidelines—not rules or laws. Apply them to your particular counseling situation according to the needs and peculiar circumstances of those involved.

1. *Communicate unconditional love and acceptance.* Persons experiencing marital difficulties and considering divorce frequently sense a rejection by friends and family. This can be devastating, for during such a trial people especially need support and encouragment. Jesus told His disciples on the night before His death, "A new commandment I give to you, that you love one another, even as I have loved you, that you also love one another" (John 13:34). The love He refers to here is not a feeling or an emotion, but rather a sacrificial commitment to another person (cf. Eph. 5:1-2). It is a love not predicated on conditions, the *agape* love which God demonstrated for us "while we were yet sinners" (Rom. 5:8).

Not only must we communicate unconditional love, but also unconditional acceptance. Paul said in Romans 15:7, "Wherefore, accept one another, just as Christ also accepted us to the glory of God." This acceptance of one another does not imply the *approval* of all a person's activities. Christ accepted us, but did not approve of our sin. We may communicate an unconditional acceptance of the people we counsel without necessarily approving all they do. *But,* those we counsel need to know that we love them unconditionally; that we accept them with their problems; and that we care enough to be personally involved with them. Such loving support is essential to the emotional stability of those in the throes of a marital breakup.

2. *Discover the root of the problem.* Divorce is really a symptom of, not a solution to, marital difficulties. Those who are considering divorce are often trying to say some-

thing to their spouse, friends or pastor about their marriage. In threatening divorce or even filing for divorce, they are saying, "I hurt; my marriage is horrible; I need help!" As a Christian counselor, one of your jobs is to help discover the root of the problem. This will take place through a process of asking probing questions and listening. Encourage the counselee to identify, elaborate and clarify his or her complaints. Question the counselee or the couple about the situations in their marriage which give rise to anger, frustration and quarrels.

Is a third person intruding in the marriage? Clyde Narramore, a noted Christian counselor, has said, "When another man or woman appears on the marriage scene, it is rarely because of an overwhelming *love*; but rather because of an overwhelming *need*."[3] Help the couple identify the needs that are not being met and that cause a partner to look to someone else to meet those needs. Discovery of the root of the problem is only partial success for the marriage counselor. Then comes the task of applying biblical principles which will provide the couple with a biblical and God-honoring solution to their difficulties.

3. *Encourage confession and forgiveness.* A marriage counselor must encourage confession and forgiveness. Not only are we to confess our sins to God (1 John 1:9), but James tells us to "confess your sins to *one another*" (James 5:16). This does not imply that we should hang our dirty laundry in the sight of all; rather, we are to admit wrong to those whom we have offended. To "confess your sins to one another" is to say, "I was wrong, and I'm sorry." Then we need to encourage the one who has been wronged to forgive (Eph. 4:32). Peter once asked Jesus, "How often shall my brother sin against me and I forgive him?" The Pharisees said that three times was enough, and so Peter doubled it, added one for good measure, and said, "Up to seven times?" Jesus replied, "No, Peter, but up to seventy times seven!" (Matt. 18:21-22). In other words, if you are still

counting, it's not enough! In view of the debt forgiven us by Christ, no sin is too great for us not to forgive one another.

Confession and forgiveness accomplish wonderful things for personal relationships. My wife, Nancy, is committed to being my wife for life. But, I sometimes carelessly or inadvertently offend her. I sin against her. That brings a "coldness" to our relationship. We are just as "married" as ever, but the joy of our companionship is gone. When I recognize my wrong, I go to her and admit that I am sorry, and I ask her forgiveness. What an amazing change takes place! Not only does our joy return, but our relationship is actually strengthened by the confession and forgiveness process. The experience actually builds bridges for further communication in our marriage. The experiences of confession and forgiveness have been some of the sweetest and most productive times in our own marriage. It is the counselor's responsibility to encourage this vital cleansing process.

4. *Instruct concerning God's plan for marriage.* The Christian counselor must also be a teacher. The counselor has the responsibility of instructing the counselee concerning God's plan for marriage as revealed in Genesis 2:24 and Ephesians 5:22-33. Start with the basics. The following outline may help you as a general guide, and chapter 1 of this book will assist you in filling in the details:

I. The Institution of Marriage (Gen. 2:24)
   A. Leaving: Separating from parents with a view to establishing a new family
   B. Cleaving: Being "glued" together in a permanent, lifelong bond
   C. Becoming One Flesh: Consummating the marriage in a physical union
II. The Obligations of Marriage (Eph. 5:22-33)
   A. The Wife: A submissive helper (Eph. 5:22)
   B. The Husband: A sacrificial lover (Eph. 5:25)

Even when counseling couples that have been married for

some time, start with the basics. Rebuild the marriage from the ground up. The biblical instruction will provide for the couple you are helping a pattern to model their marriage after.

5. *Warn concerning the consequences of divorce.* Another major responsibility of the Christian counselor is to clarify the consequences of divorce. Encourage the counselee to ask, "How will this affect my spouse?" "How will this divorce affect my children?" You may want to point out from the Scripture how God designed marriage to be a *permanent* relationship. This is implied in the word "cleave" in Genesis 2:24, and is made explicit by Jesus, "What therefore God has joined together, let no man separate" (Matt. 19:6; Mark 10:9). Four times in Paul's discussion on divorce, he sets forth the principle of "no separation" (1 Cor. 7:10-16). Since God's will is for marriage to be permanent until death, divorce is obviously not God's will. To divorce one's spouse is to elevate one's own will above God's and hence to sin a great sin (cf. 1 Sam. 15:22-23). As James declares, "Therefore, to one who knows the right thing to do, and does not do it, to him it is sin" (James 4:17).

6. *Pray for the restoration of the relationship.* An important, but often neglected, responsibility of the Christian counselor is to pray for the restoration of the marriage relationship. Since we know reconciliation is God's will as revealed in His Word, we can have great confidence that He will hear and answer our prayer (1 John 5:14-15). He may not answer at once, but that simply gives us an opportunity to demonstrate persistence. Remember the parable of the persistent petitioner in Luke 11:5-10. A man went to his friend at midnight to ask for three loaves of bread. While the friend did not want to get out of bed to answer the door, because of the persistence of the petitioner he finally got up and provided the bread. Jesus concludes the parable with, "Ask, and it shall be given to you; seek and you shall find;

knock and it shall be opened to you." Persistent prayer is not a means of "twisting God's arm," but rather His divinely appointed way of letting us communicate the measure of our desire and the greatness of our concern. We should say with Samuel as we counsel those considering divorce, "Far be it from me that I should sin against the Lord by ceasing to pray for you" (1 Sam. 12:23).

Counseling Persons Considering Remarriage

The vast majority of divorcées remarry. Various studies have shown that about 90 percent of the people who divorce enter another marriage, though probably not all of these planned to remarry at the time of divorce.[4] Since remarriage is almost inevitably a consideration for a divorced person, it is extremely important for the Christian counselor to have some guidelines to deal with those considering remarriage. Several of my guidelines overlap with the guidelines given for counseling persons considering divorce, and therefore will be considered more briefly here.

1. *Communicate unconditional love and acceptance.* Communicating unconditional love and acceptance is as essential in counseling persons considering remarriage as it is in counseling persons considering divorce. Most likely, the counselee will feel somewhat threatened even as he presents the matter of remarriage to the counselor. The counselee may be afraid that the counselor won't approve, and therefore be reluctant to open up and share. In beginning a counseling relationship communicate *agape* love—sacrificial commitment (John 13:34). Let the person you are counseling know that you accept him or her "as is," just as Christ accepted us in our own state of sin (Rom. 15:7). Such unconditional love and acceptance will form the foundation of an effective counseling relationship.

2. *Discover the counselee's personal needs.* A second major responsibility of a Christian counselor is to discover the counselee's personal needs. It is obvious that remar-

riage is expected to meet and satisfy some of these needs. Ask penetrating questions: "What are you missing in life as a single person?" "What do you see as your greatest need?" "If you could have three wishes come true, what would they be?" "How will your needs be affected by your proposed re-marriage?" Ask the questions, and then *listen attentively* for the responses! A good listener is a good counselor.

After identifying the felt needs of the counselee, I would suggest that you together "brainstorm" for creative alter-natives for meeting those needs. An ex-husband may have a need for someone to cook his meals and do his laundry. A new wife might meet the need. But a creative alternative would be to hire a maid to do the laundry once a week; per-haps he could trade off with another single person on dinner preparation. An ex-wife may feel a need for her children to have a "father image" to look up to. A new husband would possibly meet the need, but a creative alternative would be to have an uncle or church friend fill this role. Help the counselee distinguish between genuine *need* and *wants*. The desire for sexual relations may be a "want," but is it a genuine "need"? Help the counselee recognize that many "needs" are really opportunities to trust Christ's provision, or to exercise self-discipline and contentment with one's present circumstances.

3. *Instruct concerning the permanence of marriage.* A third important responsibility of the Christian counselor is to instruct concerning the permanence of marriage. Not only did Paul admonish married couples not to separate (four times in 1 Cor. 7:10-16), but he also said that marriage was broken only by death (Rom. 7:2-3; 1 Cor. 7:39). Mar-riage was designed by God to be a permanent and binding relationship until death. Only when a spouse dies is the other partner free to remarry. Divorce breaks up a home, family, and couple, but mere legal divorce does not end a marriage from God's perspective. God will end each mar-riage at His appointed time at the death of one of the mar-

riage partners (cf. Deut. 32:39; 1 Sam. 2:6).

4. *Encourage reconciliation or the single life.* The use of Scripture is an essential ingredient to Christian counseling. In ministering to divorced persons considering remarriage, the Christian counselor must lovingly confront with them the scriptural alternatives for a divorcée. The two alternatives are established by Paul in 1 Corinthians 7:11. In the case of divorce or separation the partner must either be reconciled or remain single. The option of reconciliation acknowledges the permanence of the marriage union until death (Rom. 7:2-3; 1 Cor. 7:39). The option of the single state acknowledges that remarriage to another spouse would result in adultery (Mark 10:1-12; Luke 16:18). Notice that there are only *two* options Paul gives divorced persons. Nowhere in his writings does he give permission or imply approval of remarriage for a divorced person. This truth needs to be stated lovingly but firmly to divorced persons who are considering remarriage.

5. *Warn of the consequences of remarriage.* Those who are not responsive to the scriptural options available for the divorced person need to be warned of the devastating consequences of remarriage. *First,* for a divorced person to remarry someone other than the original spouse is to commit adultery (Mark 10:1-12; Luke 16:18). *Second,* God has ordained severe consequences for those who violate His plan for marriage. In Proverbs 6:32-33 we are told:

> *The one who commits adultery with a woman is lacking sense;*
> *He who would destroy himself does it.*
> *Wounds and disgrace he will find,*
> *And his reproach will not be blotted out.*

The sin of adultery is self-destructive and brings an indelible reproach on one's name. Such a reproach would definitely diminish the spiritual effectiveness of any Christian. *Third,* Hebrews 12:6-11 reveals that God will discipline sinning Christians that they may share His holiness and yield the peaceful fruit of righteousness. Such divine discipline will not be a happy experience! *Fourth*, while the sin of adultery may be forgiven on the basis of 1 John 1:9, there will be continuing temporal consequences for those who violate God's moral law.

David is a prime example of one who inherited the *temporal* consequences of his sin. Though his sin with Bathsheba was confessed and forgiven (2 Sam. 12:13; Ps. 51), nevertheless, the child of this adulterous union died (2 Sam. 12:19). Later, David began to reap the consequences of his immorality in his own household. His daughter Tamar was raped (2 Sam 13: 1-19); his son Ammon was slain (2 Sam. 13:20-29); and his son Absolom usurped David's throne and was later killed as the rebellion was quelled (2 Sam. 15-18). Bloodshed, immorality, and rebellion marked the final years of David's reign as he sustained the consequences of his sin (2 Sam. 12:9-11). I believe God intends the temporal consequences of sin to be warnings so that others will not follow the same course of disobedience (cf. 1 Cor. 10:11).

6. *Pray for the decision of the counselee.* Finally, the Christian counselor has a responsibility to pray that the counselee will be led by the Word and the Spirit to make the proper decision concerning remarriage. Before his death, J. Edgar Hoover wrote, "The force of prayer is greater than any possible combination of man-controlled powers because prayer is man's greatest means of tapping the infinite resources of God." All too often Christians neglect this vital ministry of praying for one another. May God raise up Christian counselors whose counsel is biblical, whose hearts are tender, and whose prayers are fervent for those to whom they minister.

Summary and Conclusion

Recently as I was grading final exams, one of the seminary's recent graduates came to my office to obtain my advice on how to counsel a young man. Frank related to me how this fellow worker had trusted Christ through his ministry but was now experiencing marital difficulties. In fact, his wife had just left him. I was able to give Frank some biblical guidelines for counseling this young Christian friend, and then we bowed our heads and prayed for the restoration of this marriage.

Remember that the preceding guidelines and biblical models are suggestive rather than exhaustive. Whole books have been written on this one subject! Also remember that it is not only *what* you say, but *how* you say it that is essential to successful Christian counseling. Speak the truth as Jesus would—with confidence, conviction, and compassion. It may be the word or principle that *you* offer in love which the Lord will use to encourage some to preserve their God-ordained marriage union.

Study Questions

1. Review the biblical models for the Christian counselor. What application can you glean from Nathan's dealings with David in 2 Samuel 12?
2. What principles does Jesus' dealings with the adulterous woman in John 8 illustrate? How about His dealings with the Samaritan woman in John 4?
3. Describe the trial that the Lord took the prophet Hosea through. How do God's instructions to Hosea compare with Paul's instructions in 1 Corinthians 7:11?
4. Why is it essential for the Christian counselor to communicate an attitude of love and acceptance to persons considering divorce or remarriage?
5. Why is it important to discover the root of the marital problem in counseling a person considering divorce. How would you go about this?
6. What does confession and forgiveness accomplish for those experiencing marital difficulties?

7. What instruction from the Bible would you give a person considering divorce. Outline your answer with scripture references.

8. What instruction from the Bible would you give a divorced person considering remarriage? Outline your answer with scripture references.

9. What consequences of divorce and remarriage are spelled out for us in the Word of God?

Notes

1. Reader's Digest Almanac, 1981, p. 415.

2. Zane Hodges, "The Woman Taken in Adultery (John 7:53-8:11): The Text," *Bibliotheca Sacra* (October-December, 1979), pp. 318-332; A. Johnson, "A Stylistic Trait of the Fourth Gospel in the *Pericope Adulterae*," *Bulletin of the Evangelical Theological Society* (Spring 1966), pp. 91-96; A. Trites, "The Woman Taken in Adultery," *Bibliotheca Sacra* (April-June, 1974), pp. 137-46.

3. Clyde M. Narramore, *The Psychology of Counseling* (Grand Rapids: Zondervan Publishing House, 1960), p. 202.

4. John R. Martin, *Divorce and Remarriage: A Perspective for Counseling* (Scottdale, Pennsylvania: Herald Press, 1974), p. 111.

12

Restoring God's Standard

In a recent edition of the *Oregon Journal*, the Portland evening newspaper, I noticed the following classified ad:

DIVORCE SERVICE

$58.00

All legal fees and services
included in the one low price.

Phone 234-1000

What a bargain! Your marriage can be legally dissolved for a mere 58 dollars—just a day's wage for many people. This advertisement tells me several things about marriage and divorce in our modern society. *First*, to many people, marriage is cheap. It is a relationship that is casually entered into and inexpensively dissolved. Hundreds of people will respond to this advertisement and throw their marriages away for the price of a good pair of shoes! *Second*, divorce is easy. The "no fault" divorce of recent times eliminates the necessity of proving one member to be "the guilty party." If the divorce is uncontested, the marriage may be easily nullified. Divorce in such a situation is almost a clerical legal procedure. *Third*, divorce is rampant! It is the old case of "supply and demand." Because of the public demand for quick and easy divorce, accommodating lawyers have provided divorce services almost on the scale of an assembly line to meet the need and to make a dollar. What a tragic commentary on marriage and the family in America is the little advertisement, "Divorce Service—$58.00." Fallen man has certainly deviated a long way from God's original plan for marriage. The church must hold up God's standard for the world to see.

As we draw our study to a conclusion, it would be helpful to summarize and briefly apply the doctrine, and make several concluding comments. We have come a long way in our study, having carefully examined the crucial biblical texts relating to the issues of divorce and remarriage. Think with me now as we take some time for review.

The Doctrine Summarized

1. Marriage is a human relationship ordained and instituted by God. While the laws of the land and marriage customs vary in different cultures, marriage involves basically three elements: (1) a public act expressing the intent of the couple, (2) a permanent bonding of two lives together, and (3) a physical union consummating the relationship (Gen. 2:24).

2. God's original design for marriage was one man united with one wife for life (Gen. 2:23-24; 5:2). It is not His desire that there be any divorce (Matt. 19:6; Mark 10:9).

3. Neither God nor Moses *commanded* that there be divorce. Divorce was taking place due to man's rejection of the original divine plan for marriage, so to protect the rights of the rejected wife God required that the woman being divorced be provided a bill of divorcement (Deut. 24:1-4).

4. The divorcement required by Ezra and Nehemiah was a unique attempt on the part of these leaders of the restoration community to keep the messianic line pure and the Hebrew faith uncontaminated as a result of mixed marriages with idolatrous Gentiles (Ezra 9-10; Neh. 13:23-30). Any attempt to apply these passages to modern marriage

would contradict the teaching of Paul who commanded believers not to initiate divorce against an unbelieving spouse (1 Cor. 7:12-16).

5. God hates divorce because it is a treacherous violation of a covenant relationship and contrary to His original plan for marriage (Mal. 2:14-16; Gen. 2:24). Jesus' explanation for God tolerating divorce in the Old Testament period is the hardness of the people's hearts—hearts set against God's will and Word (Matt. 19:8; Mark 10:5).

6. Both Jesus and the apostle Paul taught the principle of no divorce (Matt. 5:31-32; 19:1-12; Mark 10:1-12; Luke 16:18; 1 Cor. 7:10-16). Divorce and remarriage results in adultery, the only exception being in the case of marriage within the forbidden degrees of kinship (Lev. 18:6-18).

7. Since death breaks the marriage bond (Rom. 7:2-3; 1 Cor. 7:39), remarriage is permissible without sin for a believing widow or widower, if the marriage is with another believer (1 Cor. 7:39; 2 Cor. 6:14-18).

8. In the case of divorce, there are only two options available for the divorced person: (1) to remain permanently in an unmarried state, or (2) be reconciled to one's partner (1 Cor. 7:11).

9. The pastor/elder and deacon of the New Testament church must be "the husband of one wife"—married just once. One who is divorced or divorced and remarried would be disqualified. A man who is not totally devoted to his one wife and is in the habit of lusting after other women would also be disqualified from the church offices of elder and deacon (1 Tim. 3:2, 12; Titus 1:6).

The Doctrine Applied

While an entire chapter has already been devoted to the application of the biblical doctrine of divorce and remarriage, you may find the following chart helpful for review or future reference (see pages 148-149):

THE SITUATION	THE SIN	THE SCRIPTURE	THE SOLUTION
1. Divorce	Violation of a covenant relationship and contrary to God's plan for marriage	Mal. 2:14 Gen. 2:24 Matt. 19:6 Mark 10:9	* Confess sin (1 John 1:9) * Work for reconciliation (1 Cor. 7:11) * If reconciliation is not possible, remain single for life (1 Cor. 7:11)
a. For unfaithfulness	Misinterpretation of the exception clause; failure to forgive sin	Matt. 5:32 19:9 Eph. 4:32	* Forgive the unfaithful partner (Matt. 6:14-15; Eph. 4:32) * Be reconciled in the marriage (1 Cor. 7:11)
b. For desertion	Misinterpretation of the phrase "not under bondage"	1 Cor. 7:15	* Forgive the deserter (Matt. 6:14-15) * Be reconciled in the relationship (1 Cor. 7:11)
2. Remarriage a. Contemplated	Sin of adultery under consideration	Mark 10:11-12	* Flee such immorality (2 Tim. 2:22) * Do not go through with the marriage (James 4:17)
b. Consummated	Sin of adultery	Mark 10:11-12 Luke 16:18	* Confess the sin (1 John 1:9) * Maintain the marriage (1 Cor. 7:10-11)
3. Divorce & Remarriage (before or after remarriage)	Sin of adultery	Mark 10:11-12 Luke 16:18	* Confess sin (1 John 1:9) * Recognize forgiveness (Rom. 5:1; 8:1)

			* Distinguish between forgiveness of sin and consequences of sin (1 John 1:9; Gal. 6:7)
4. Marriage to a divorced person	Sin of adultery	Luke 16:18	* Confess the sin (1 John 1:9) * Recognize forgiveness (Rom. 5:1; 8:1) * Realize limitations in Christian service (1 Tim. 3:2, 12; Titus 1:6)
5. Divorce, new marriage, remarriage	To return to a former spouse after an intervening marriage is an abomination to the Lord	Deut. 24:1-4	* Confess the sin (1 John 1:9) * Avoid such sin (2 Tim. 2:22) * Do not break up a second marriage to return to a former spouse (1 Cor. 7:10-11)
6. Endangered wife	Husband threatens wife physically; her life is endangered	1 Cor. 7:11	* If separation is unavoidable, remain single and work toward reconciliation (1 Cor. 7:11)
7. Divorced and remarried candidate for elder or deacon	Not "above reproach" nor a "husband of one wife"	1 Tim. 3:2, 12 Titus 1:6	* Realize that sin may disqualify one from certain opportunities of service (1 Sam. 15:22-23) * Encourage the candidate to use his gifts in some capacity other than the office of elder or deacon

Concluding Remarks

In a sense, one never concludes the study of any Bible doctrine. Further light may be shed on many of the Bible's teachings through modern archaeological excavation, studies in historical backgrounds, and careful exegesis. Clarifications and more precise statements of doctrine can be made as students of the Bible stand on the shoulders of past generations of scholars and reach further into the Word for God's truth. But, for the purposes of our present study we have reached the end of our investigation.

We have found that the teaching of the Bible on the subject of divorce and remarriage is quite strict when compared with the accepted norms of American society. God's original design for marriage was for one man to be united with one woman for life. Divorce resultantly occurred when man rejected God's plan, but God has never changed the ideal. Nowhere in Scripture does God lower His righteous standards to accommodate man's fallen nature, even under grace. Through Moses God regulated divorce and through Paul He regulated slavery (Eph. 6:5-9; Col. 3:22-4:1), but in no way did God institute either of these evils. God's hatred of divorce is reflected in the teachings of Jesus and Paul who both viewed the marriage union as indissoluble except by death. Only two options remain for divorced persons: (1) to remain permanently in an unmarried state, or (2) be reconciled to one's partner.

Realizing that teachers are responsible for the accuracy of their doctrine and will be judged for leading others into error (Matt. 18:6-7; Heb. 13:17; James 3:1), I have sought to reflect in this book what the Bible teaches concerning divorce and remarriage. I trust that by careful study and God's enabling grace I have accomplished that objective.

I believe God will bless our churches when teachers, pastors, and Christian workers hold to the biblical doctrine of the permanence of marriage until death. Only then will

Christian marriage accurately picture the indissoluble relationship between Christ and His church. May we as Christians obey the teaching of Jesus concerning the permanence
of marriage, not because we fully understand or appreciate
this truth, but because we love Him who said, "If you love
Me, you will keep My commandments" (John 14:15).

Review Questions

1. What is marriage from a biblical point of view (Gen.
   2:24)? Explain in your own words why God instituted the marriage relationship.
2. What roles has God given a husband and wife in
   marriage (Eph. 5:22-30)? Does submission suggest
   inferiority? Explain your answer.
3. What would you identify as the main point of the
   legislation given by Moses in Deuteronomy 24:1-4?
   According to Matthew 19:8 and Mark 10:5, why did
   God tolerate divorce among His people?
4. Why did the leaders of the restoration community
   require divorce as recorded in Ezra 9-10 and Nehemiah 13:23-30? Would it be right to make application of these passages to modern marriage (1 Cor.
   7:12-13)?
5. What is God's attitude toward divorce (Mal.
   2:10-16)? What is His attitude toward divorced persons? How is your evaluation of traditional atti-
   tudes toward divorced persons? What changes
   would you suggest?
6. What argument does Jesus use in Mark 10:6-9 to
   demonstrate that divorce is actually alien to God's
   plan for marriage?
7. What unique contribution does Matthew 19:1-12
   make concerning Jesus' teaching on divorce and remarriage? What unique contribution is found in
   Mark 10:11-12? How about Luke 16:18?

8. What are the possible interpretations of the exception clause in Matthew 5:32 and 19:9? Which do you believe has the best support? Present a summary of the evidence for your view.

9. According to the teaching of Paul, what terminates a marriage relationship before God (Rom. 7:2-3; 1 Cor. 7:39)? What light does this shed on the instruction Paul gives divorced persons in 1 Corinthians 7:11?

10. Does 1 Corinthians 7:15 teach that divorce and remarriage is permitted in the case of desertion? Why not? What key interpretive principle helps us understand this verse?

11. What is the meaning of the phrase "the husband of one wife" as Paul uses it in 1 Timothy 3:2, 12 and Titus 1:6 where he sets forth the qualifications for elder and deacon? Why do you think it would be important for a church leader to meet this qualification.

12. What steps can be taken in your church to discourage divorce and instruct people on the permanence of the marriage bond for life? Formulate some plans for helping teenagers, young couples, and mature adults gain God's perspective on marriage.

Selective Bibliography

Adams, Jay. E. *Marriage, Divorce and Remarriage*. Presbyterian and Reformed Publishing Company, 1980.

Boice, James Montgomery. "The Biblical View of Divorce." *Eternity* 21 (December 1970), pp. 19-21.

Clarke, W. K. Lowther. "The Exception Clause in St. Matthew." *Theology* 15 (1927), pp. 161-62.

————. *New Testament Problems*. New York: Macmillan, 1929.

Coiner, H. G. "Those 'Divorce and Remarriage' Passages (Matt. 5:32; 19:9; 1 Cor. 7:10-16)." *Concordia Theological Monthly* 39 (June 1968), pp. 367-84.

DeHaan, Richard W. *Marriage, Divorce, and Remarriage*. Grand Rapids: Radio Bible Class, 1979.

Duty, Guy. *Divorce and Remarriage*. Minneapolis, Minnesota: Bethany Fellowship, Inc., 1967.

Ellisen, Stanley A. *Divorce and Remarriage in the Church*. Grand Rapids: Zondervan Publishing House, 1977.

Evans, William. *The Right and Wrong in Divorce and Remarriage*. Grand Rapids: Zondervan Publishing House, 1946.

Fisher-Hunter, W. *Marriage and Divorce*. Waynesboro, Pennsylvania: MacNeish Publishers, 1952.

Fitzmyer, Joseph A. "The Matthean Divorce Texts and Some New Palestinian Evidence." *Theological Studies* 37 (1976), pp. 213-21.

Martin, John R. *Divorce and Remarriage: A perspective for Counseling*. Scottdale, Pennsylvania: Herald Press, 1974.

Murray, John. *Divorce*. Philadelphia: Orthodox Presbyterian Church, 1953.

Ryrie, Charles C. *The Role of Women in the Church*. Chicago: Moody Press, 1970.

————. *You Mean the Bible Teaches That*. Chicago: Moody Press, 1974.

Saucy, Robert L. "The Husband of One Wife." *Bibliotheca Sacra* 131 (July-September, 1974), pp. 229-40.

Small, Dwight Hervey. *The Right to Remarry*. Old Tappan, New Jersey: Fleming H. Revel Company, 1975.

Stein, Robert H. "Is It Lawful for a Man to Divorce His Wife?" *Journal of the Evangelical Theological Society* 22 (June 1979), pp. 115-21.

Telford, Andrew. *The Miscarriage of Marriage*. Tampa, Florida: Grace Publishing Company, Inc., 1975.

Vawter, Bruce. "The Divorce Clauses in Matthew 5:32 and 19:9." *Catholic Biblical Quarterly* (April 1954), pp. 155-76.

Scripture Index

Topical Index